Charanik

Mohonlal Gangopadhyay (19 August 1909–14 January 1969) was an eminent writer of a number of very popular books, some of which are still widely read. His travel books, including *Charanik*, *Lafa Yatra* and *Punardarshanaya Cho*, are still in print, as are *Dakshiner Baranda* and *Gaganendranath*.

He had also written stories for young people, notably *Galpodadar Galpo*; a few other stories were compiled into the volume *Kishor Rachana Sangraha*. He also produced a study of the jute industry, titled *Asamapta Chatabda*. In addition, he published Bengali translations of *Grimm's Fairy Tales* and Erich Maria Remarque's classic *All Quiet on the Western Front*.

Jayanta Sengupta worked in advertising for many years, before deciding to leave the corporate world and take up things that he couldn't earlier. Being a voracious reader all his life, he started to dabble in writing. His first book, *WrapAround: Delivering a Great Brand Experience* (Rupa Publications, 2006), was about designing and delivering great brand experiences.

In 2011, his translation of Bibhutibhushan Bandopadhyay's Bengali classic *Chander Pahar* was published by Rupa as *The Mountain of the Moon*.

This book is his second translation and his third book published under the Rupa banner. *Charanik: The Walker* is a travel classic by Mohonlal Gangopadhyay, which was first published in 1961.

Also by the author

WrapAround: Delivering a Great Brand Experience
The Mountain of the Moon

The Walker

MOHONLAL GANGOPADHYAY

Translated by *Jayanta Sengupta*

RUPA

Published by
Rupa Publications India Pvt. Ltd 2021
7/16, Ansari Road, Daryaganj
New Delhi 110002

Sales centres:
Allahabad Bengaluru Chennai
Hyderabad Jaipur Kathmandu
Kolkata Mumbai

Copyright © Urmila Ganguli and Mitendra Ganguli 2021
Translation copyright © Jayanta Sengupta 2021

Photographs and artworks courtesy Urmila Ganguli and Mitendra Ganguli

All rights reserved.
No part of this publication may be reproduced, transmitted,
or stored in a retrieval system, in any form or by any means,
electronic, mechanical, photocopying, recording or otherwise,
without the prior permission of the publisher.

The views and opinions expressed in this book are
the author's own and the facts are as reported by him
which have been verified to the extent possible,
and the publishers are not in any way liable for the same.

ISBN: 978-81-291-4502-4

First impression 2021

10 9 8 7 6 5 4 3 2 1

Printed at Thomson Press India Ltd, Faridabad

This book is sold subject to the condition that it shall not,
by way of trade or otherwise, be lent, resold, hired out, or otherwise
circulated, without the publisher's prior consent, in any form of
binding or cover other than that in which it is published.

INTRODUCTIONS BY THE AUTHOR

To the First Edition

Through woods and forests, through fields and meadows, I've travelled on foot in many countries. I've enjoyed every single minute of it, and in this book, I've tried to share this joy with others. Of course, it is difficult to vicariously explain the joys of journeying on foot to those who have never done so themselves. However, I really do hope that this account of my journeys will inspire some readers to take a few sips from the chalice of joy that walking tours can bring.

There are hundreds and thousands of people in our country who travel long distances on foot, braving the many risks, hazards and hardships of the road. Most of them are pilgrims going from one sacred shrine to another, undertaking severe acts of penance and suffering without complaint. But the walker I have in mind is not a pilgrim; he is a student, who wishes to see the world and experience its myriad beauties while he's still young. This young man finds it very difficult to wander about the forests and mountain peaks in our land. Such journeys become particularly difficult when there are very few places to spend the nights. Of course, travellers on foot cannot be lazybones or care overmuch about their creature comforts, but why should the pleasures of a walking tour be confined only to the adventurous and to those who can handle the hardships of the road?

In Europe, the Youth Hostels Association has solved the problem of finding shelters for the night in a marvellous way. People like me who have spent days and nights walking through the lanes and bylanes of the Himalayas really believe that similar solutions are needed in our country, even if they are started in a small way.

To the Second Edition

The incidents described in *Charanik* took place in 1937. I wrote the book in 1942. The current edition contains some materials which have been retrieved from the pages of my old diaries.

TRANSLATOR'S NOTE

Charanik has been a favourite of mine since my school days. For some good deed that I had committed in my early teens, my school gave it to me as a prize, suitably inscribed. My good deed has been long forgotten, but the reward has been highly valued, cherished and perused every few years. It had had a longer-term effect on my own holidays in Europe, to which I shall return later.

Mohonlal Gangopadhyay came from a very illustrious family. His father was the highly esteemed litterateur Manilal Gangopadhyay, and his mother, Karuna, was the daughter of Abanindranath Tagore. Mohonlal Gangopadhyay has indelibly captured his childhood with his grandfather and two granduncles—Gaganendranath and Samarendranath Tagore—in a wonderful book called *Dakshiner Baranda* (this could be rendered in English as *The Southern Verandah* or *The Porch on the South*).

Mr Gangopadhyay studied at Hare School and Presidency College, Kolkata, and at the London School of Economics, UK. He later joined the Indian Statistical Institute, Kolkata, at the invitation of its founder, P.C. Mahalanobis. I remember that Mr Gangopadhyay's wife, Milada, taught in my school, South Point in Kolkata, for those who are interested—

although I have no recollection of ever having been in her class.

As the author mentions in his introductions, the travels described in this book took place in the summer of 1937. The reader will recall that by that time, Adolf Hitler was already in power in Germany and the Nazis were planning for the expansion of German territory by creating Lebensraum ('living space') for the German people, as documented in the Hossbach Memorandum. The Germans in Czechoslovakia (Sudetenland) were demanding the right to autonomy, which led directly to the Munich Pact being signed between Hitler and Neville Chamberlain in September 1938; as a result, parts of Czechoslovakia would be handed over to Nazi Germany. The Anschluss (occupation) of Austria would take place in March 1938. The German army would invade Poland on 1 September 1939, England would declare war on Germany on 3 September 1939 and the Second World War would commence. It is, of course, a matter of history that war had been in the air in Europe for some years before 1939.

Yet, none of these events and their effects is reflected in this book. The Czechoslovakia described is idyllic, peaceful and beautiful. The only concern of the Mireks and the Pepeks (like the brothers Mirek and Pepek in this book) is their journey and the important matters of food, road and shelter. It is refreshing to read of a wonderful world which its people could enjoy at an apocalyptic period in human history.

When I decided to visit Europe in the early 1980s—alone the first time and two years later with my wife—I decided to do so with shoestring *Charanik*-like budget. I learnt about youth hostels from this book, which also gave me an idea of food, drink and shelter on the cheap; my wife and I became members of the Youth Hostels Association and its cards gave us many benefits, all welcome to tourists who are trying to 'do' Europe in low double-digit dollars a day.

The Association is now called the European Union Federation of Youth Hostel Associations (EUFED) and the interested traveller can find out more about this at http://www.eufed.org.

The map of Czechoslovakia, like a lot of Central Europe, has changed drastically over the last few decades. Czechoslovakia separated into the Czech Republic and Slovakia. Slovenia came into existence as an independent nation. Ruthenia had not really existed as an independent state. Quite a few of the places referred to in this book can now be found in the maps of Hungary, Poland, Ukraine and other countries.

In trying to give the local spellings of place names as accurately as I could, I've referred to Google Maps and other online sources. It is quite likely that there are errors in the spellings, for which I plead guilty, with ignorance of local languages as my excuse. However, the reader may well find that his or her enjoyment of the narrative is not likely to be affected by incorrect spellings of place names—at least that's what I hope.

In some chapters, I have included lines from local songs that the author has quoted in the Bengali original. I have been able to provide translations in some cases, thanks to various sources. In one case, I have not been able to do so.

I couldn't even figure out the language it was in! It is quite likely that there will be errors in my inexpert attempts at translations, and I offer my apologies in advance.

In this work, I have used the terms 'rupee' or 'rupees' for the Indian currency instead of the symbol. The original uses these terms and, in any case, the symbol was introduced many decades after the events of the book.

The concluding line of the final chapter, i.e., 'If, rather, I had been an Arab Bedouin...' is from the famous poem 'Duranta Asha' ('Desperate Hope') by Rabindranath Tagore. In Bengali script, the rendering is extremely popular:

ইহার চেয়ে হতেম যদি আরব বেদুয়িন!
(Ihar cheye hotem jodi Arab Bedouin!)

The English translation that I have used is from https://www.indoindians.com/duranta-asha/.

For this translation, I have used the book that my school gave me, published by Bengal Publishers Private Limited, Calcutta, in Ashar, 1367 as per the Bengali calendar (June 1960 in the Gregorian calendar). It's very gratifying to know that the author's travel books are available as a single volume in Bengali, ensuring that these are available to newer generations of readers. Perhaps these books will inspire other young men and women to throw their bare necessities into a rucksack, hit the road and travel the world on foot and a thin wallet.

ONE

*I*n this day and age, if I were to express a desire to walk from Calcutta to Uttarpara instead of taking a bus or a train, most people will look askance at me, thinking that there's something wrong inside my head. Why Calcutta to Uttarpara? Let's consider a much shorter distance, say from Maniktola to Beniapukur. Only the very poorest person will willingly think about walking such a distance. And it's not as if only the really poor travel from one place to another on foot. Quite often, you can see a sadhu sitting on a tiger-skin cushion in a third-class carriage of a train in India—you can be sure that he has not bought any ticket for his pilgrim's progress!

Nowadays, it is very rare to find people who walk from Puri to Dwarka, from Dwarka to Setubandha Rameshwaram, and similar long journeys from one place of pilgrimage to another. You will find such hardy and intrepid souls only on the really dangerous routes like the road to Manasarovar or the paths to Kedarnath and Badrinath.

From time to time, we still come across interesting tales of people who have traversed long distances on foot. Some time ago, a gentleman in Bombay suddenly lost his job. He knocked on many doors for a new job, without any success. Things became serious—it was becoming well-nigh impossible to make ends meet. Through a sense of desperation, he started walking east from Bombay along the railway lines. After many days and weeks, he reached Nagpur, where the gods of fortune suddenly smiled upon him. A European heard about his travails, bought him a ticket and sent him on to Calcutta, where he got a job. Thereafter, he probably did not go for any long walk.

Some time ago, I met an Englishman in Calcutta. He left his homeland four years ago and walked through Europe, Turkey and Iran and reached India. The only time he did not walk was when he took boats to cross rivers and seas. He had walked across most of India by the time he reached Calcutta.

When I met him, he was planning to walk to the hills of Darjeeling, thereafter to Assam, and then through the forests of Assam to Burma and then on to China. From China, he planned to travel by sea to America, and after he was done walking through America, get on board a ship to go back home. He expected to spend three more years on the road.

In a long conversation, he shared many interesting and exciting stories about his encounters on the road.

He had walked through the forests of Mysore for many days, forests which are bewitchingly beautiful but can be terribly dangerous. These forests are home to many ferocious animals, most dangerous of which are tigers. During the day, my intrepid friend used to walk with his gun on his shoulder, fully aware that tigers were following his movements from the shelter of bushes and undergrowth. However, for whatever reason, tigers never attacked him, and he had never had to fire his gun.

When I asked him where he spent the nights, he said, 'Next to the forest path.'

'Weren't you scared of tigers?' I asked.

'Not at all. Tigers prefer to attack a moving target; I don't believe that they will harm an animal that is standing still or lying down. Thanks to this conviction, I can still snore peacefully at night in the forests, and indeed am still alive and well. But, I don't trust your snakes. I always spread a thick rope made from coir all around my jungle bed, and then I can sleep in peace. A snake won't go over such a rope—they are rough, and will prick the snake's soft skin.'

There have always been such spirited adventurous walkers everywhere in the world. In addition, there are the walkers of today, who walk from one village to another, from one village market to another, with their wares. But if you leave aside these exceptions, you'll find that most people do not walk any more. There are now so many means of travel, that there is no need to walk long distances any more.

It's true that people in our country have to walk a lot more than their counterparts in the West, where amenities to travel like roads, trains, airplanes and other modes are more widely available; we are not as well provided in this regard. In India, we have towns and villages so far apart that to go from one village to another, people have no option but to walk for miles and miles.

Conditions were almost the same in Europe. I am talking about a time when the railways had not been invented, let alone the motor car. The only mode of long-distance travel available to the general public was horse-drawn carriages, which also carried mail. In those days, the roads were not as broad and well-made as those you find today; they were narrow, winding, filled with ridges, ditches and potholes. The rich travelled in their own carriages. The affluent class, who did not keep their own carriages, travelled in the post carriages I've mentioned. They would travel for a hundred miles or more, changing post carriages on the way; this was considered a courageous way of going from one place to another and was supposed to be quite an adventure. If they came back from their journeys without breaking an arm or a leg, and without being attacked by dacoits and highwaymen, they considered themselves really fortunate.

That was the state of the affluent. What about the poor? They did not have the wherewithal to afford post carriages, so they did not travel at all and spent their entire lives in their own villages and nearby areas. There were many places in Europe, particularly in Germany, where, for many generations, the residents never stepped outside the walls of their towns. They had no contact with and no news from the outside world. One such place is the famous city of Nürnberg. If you visit Nürnberg today, you will still find the fortifications and stone towers of the old town.

At one time, a guild of wonderful singers from within the walled city created a special style of writing lyric poetry, composition and unaccompanied art song. They did not allow outside influences to affect their art form. Tales of their orthodoxy and obstinacy have been well told in a very famous opera called *The Meistersinger of Nürnberg*, composed by Richard Wagner.

Another such town is Rothenburg, whose massive high walls have been preserved even today. The whole town has been kept exactly as it used to be in the past. The fortifications, the streets and lanes, the houses, their roofs, doors and windows, the shops—nothing has been allowed to change since the heydays of the town. One wonders how the townspeople used to lead their entire lives inside the walls of its massive medieval fortifications.

At a time when many people in Europe used to spend their lives in such an unchanging environment, there was a group of people who travelled from one country to another on foot. These were university students. They would hear of the fame of some far-away university and want to pursue their further studies there. They were no different from the students who came from far away to learn at the school of Sri Chaitanya at Nabadwip.

The European students were not rich. So, they would walk from Paris to Rome, Rome to Prague and Prague to Heidelberg in search of knowledge. It took them several months to complete their journeys, and on the way, they would pass through many villages and towns and meet and converse with people from different countries and many walks of life. Such an experience was not in any way inferior to the knowledge they would acquire in a university. Thanks to the travelling bands of students, many parts of Europe did not stagnate and become rigid.

Until the railways were invented and the railway system

was created, the students of Europe kept alive the tradition of walking. Of course, this was difficult and sometimes dangerous, but it was fun, exciting and most importantly educational as well.

Then came the railways, followed by the motor car and the electric train. Railway lines covered the land; wide and well-constructed roads were built. The railway tracks and the roads connected not just cities and towns in one country but across countries as well. Finally came the aeroplane. Much before its arrival, however, university students had given up their practice of walking from one place to another. Nowadays, if a mathematics student in Paris wishes to study astronomy from an expert in Berlin, he will never even dream of going there on foot. In these days of mechanization, it would be considered madness

Surprisingly, the 'madness' of walking long distances has returned in Europe, about 25 years ago. In the past, people travelled on foot for some reason or the other; now, they do so for the sake of walking. The attraction of walking is no longer limited to university students alone: students of all descriptions as well as others from widely different walks of life have also found the joy and excitement of walking.

Let me tell you how and why this happened.

TWO

When the World War ended in 1918, Europe was in a very bad state, and Europeans were disgusted and embittered with the modern mechanized world that had made such destruction possible.

Germany was devastated. They had lost the war; there was a severe shortage of money, food and other basic necessities. The man on the street had a very difficult time trying to keep himself and his family fed, clothed and amused.

Before the war, students enjoyed themselves in cinemas, theatres, cabarets, carnivals, dance halls, night clubs and 'bierstubes' (or taverns). After the war, however, such ways of amusement seemed trivial and meaningless. Besides, there was no money to afford such pleasures. Of course young people need fun and amusement in their lives, but it has to be natural, easily available and, most of all, cheap.

People had forgotten that walking could be fun too. Until one day, people in Germany noticed that a group of boys and girls, with shoulder packs, were out walking. Today, leaving home on a trip costs a lot of money; you have to spend nights out, which means hotel expenses, cost of food, and also tips and gratuities to a lot of people.

These kids had very little money, so they gave up the

idea of staying in hotels and eating in restaurants. In fact, they avoided towns and cities altogether; instead, they walked from one tiny village to another. They found shelter for the night, at very little cost, in the attics of cottages of the villagers, used for storing hay and feed for their horses. Some carried tents in their rucksacks and made their beds on leaves in pine woods. To save money on food, they carried stoves in their packs and a few simple utensils to prepare their food in. Certainly all this added to the weight on their shoulders, but it was a lot more fun than staying in hotels, or travelling by rail. How to spend nights in villages at the least possible cost and what to eat while resting under trees, next to a stream, at the lowest cost—all this became quite a field of study among these young people.

Soon, more and more young people joined in. Quickly, they discovered the joy of leaving home and spending their time travelling from one pretty little village to another, climbing one beautiful hill after another, traversing one magnificent pine forest after another, cooking their own simple meals, making their own beds, putting up their tents, all the while carrying heavy loads on their shoulders. From one end of Germany to the other, boys and girls in large numbers became expert walkers. They were soon named 'Wandervogel' or 'wandering bird'.

Very soon, this became a very popular movement and it spread from Germany to other countries in Europe and also to England. In many countries, the members of the movement formed organizations to look after their needs. Membership fees were minimal, but when a lot of members got together, the fees were quite significant and could accomplish a lot. The most important use for the money was to provide places for hikers to stay at very low cost, and small cottages, similar to the dak bungalows in India, were built. There was nothing luxurious or refined about these—there was no need for that and no money anyway. There were old unused houses, cottages, small factories and thatched sheds all over the country—all of which were very useful. The organization bought some of these at very low prices, while some were donated by their kind and generous owners. Some quick repairs, a lick of paint, and soon they were ready as shelters for the walkers.

Naturally, these cottages were most numerous at places most frequently visited by walkers. On the longer routes between cottages, new cottages had to be built, just like the inns and taverns at intervals on long roads between cities. Slowly, the whole country was covered by a network of such cottages for the foot travellers.

The organizations came to be known as Youth Hostels Association and the cottages were called Youth Hostels. Germany has 2,000 such hostels, England has about 300, and even a small country like Denmark has 200.

Staying overnight at these hostels is very cheap, particularly if you are a member of the association. Each hostel has a common kitchen, where you can cook yourself a meal. Some hostels also have canteens, where one can buy food at a very low cost.

Over time, members of the Youth Hostels Association of one country established relationships with those of other countries and, as a result, members of the association in one country started to use the facilities of associations in other countries.

As a result, the walking tourists of today do not face much difficulties in Europe. Not only can they travel in their own countries at a minimal cost, but they can walk through other countries as well with ease and comfort. Today, if you go to Europe in summer, you will find large groups of youthful walkers with rucksacks, walking on village paths, through fields, particularly in the hills and mountains.

These are the spontaneous, natural, joyful and young people of Europe today.

THREE

I knew nothing of all this when I went to Europe. I had read an essay on the Wandervogel in *Mouchak* magazine, years ago, and I had imagined the average walker to be a tough, hardy and dauntless person. Not me, I thought. How I became a walker, quickly, easily and suddenly, is the story of this book.

I studied in London. There were no classes on weekends and I don't recall having touched my books on weekends during my first year of college. When I was studying in Calcutta, I was very often at a loss as to how to pass my time during the off days. London posed no such problems—there were many things that the city offered during holidays. I went to the theatre, concerts, clubs, museums, lectures, trips, parties and countless other indulgences.

That was only for Saturdays and Sundays. In addition, there were the vacations during Christmas, Easter and the long summer break. During Christmas, London offered a variety of things to keep you busy and entertained. One could fill up part of the Easter holidays with some studies, but it was a vacation anyway and towards the end of the period, it was really difficult to fill up time with one's textbooks and academic work; my memory tells me that it was pretty boring towards the end of the break.

Then came the long three-month summer vacation. I had appeared for the annual examination and was confident of passing, hence there was no opportunity, nor need, to fill up time with studies. I was bored of going to clubs, parties and the theatre. What to do with my time became quite a burning problem.

I decided that I shall not spend it in the city—I shall travel and, if possible, go to a distant country.

A few weeks later, a friend wrote to me from Germany with a very tempting offer.

> Fly like a swan and join me here. A shiny new bicycle is waiting for you. We shall cycle through all of Germany, all over Austria and also travel through northern Italy and see the well-known sights in these beautiful countries. We shall travel together and perhaps we shall be joined on our journey by other like-minded travellers. The pleasant warmth of summer in the continent is like the tender touch of a soft, scented hand. The billowing fields of Germany are awash with the blossoms of the Alpine Marguerite; the woods are filled with all imaginable hues of green. The snows of the hills and mountains have melted and emerged as springs, rills, streams and rivers. After the silence of winter, the cuckoo has given tongue. Birds that have been silent all this time are filling the air with endless songs.

Such was the tenor of my friend's letter—an invitation that I found very tempting, almost irresistible. On the other hand, I had reservations about going on a bike tour with my friend. For one thing, he was a well-built guy—tough and strong; he's likely to ride his bike at such a pace that it would be hard to keep up with him. Second, riding on a bicycle meant travelling on highways, with cars, trucks and buses for company. Third, my friend wanted to visit big cities like Berlin, Munich, Vienna, Milan and Rome, and I had not the slightest desire to see those places.

I had planned to stay away from the noise and the crowds of cities; I wanted to mingle with the rural people of the country I visited; I wanted to see and participate in the songs, dances, tales and jokes of the countryfolk.

In London, I had made friends with a person who loved travelling. He was from Czechoslovakia and had since gone back home. He had shown me many pictures of the beautiful mountains and magnificent vistas of his homeland. So, I decided to finalize my travel plans after talking to my friend. Czechoslovakia was also quite far from London. My plan was to not make a fixed itinerary. I would visit one place, stay on for as long as I liked, and then move on to the next by train, bus or anything else that I could get on, until the end of my holidays.

Nowadays, Czechoslovakia is a part of Germany and getting permission to enter is virtually impossible. But I am writing about a time when it was still independent and posed no problems of entering or leaving the country. Without wasting much time, I quickly made arrangements and boarded a train to Prague, the capital of Czechoslovakia.

From England, across Germany to Prague was a journey

of 36 hours. The first thing was to meet my friend. 'Mirek, I have come to see your country,' I said. 'Not to see the cities and museums, like tourists. I want to see the villages, the countryside, the mountains, the natural beauty of your land. I want to meet the villagers, and stay far away from railway lines and highways.'

Mirek jumped at my plan. 'Wonderful!' he exclaimed. 'My holidays have started, and I was also thinking of travelling in my homeland. Take me with you. Let's do it together.'

I explained that I had come to him to learn about the places to visit.

Mirek said, 'Let us find out about that.'

He took me to the Klub Československých Turistů (Czechoslovakian Tourist Club). Mirek studied the big maps, pictures and books at the club, and I learnt many wonderful things about Czechoslovakia. Mirek told me that the places to visit in Czechoslovakia are the mountains. First, the Tatra Mountains, with their sharp-pointed peaks, teeming with lakes and streams, lined with Alpine flowers. People come from all over the world to see the beauty of the Tatras. Second, the Carpathian Mountains, with its primeval forests covering hundreds of acres, where it is believed that the feet of men has not touched the ground for centuries.

I took notes of such pieces of information and then we made a rough plan, which we would follow with the proviso of making changes as and when we felt like. We decided to leave for Slovakia in the next couple of days.

My friend had advised me to become a member of the Tourist Club. The annual membership was only about two rupees, but the benefits were worth more than two hundred rupees. A member gets an identification card with his photograph, which entitles him to discounts on trains, as well as on tickets to theatres, the opera, museums and many other places of interest. Many shops also charge lower prices to members. The club brings out a monthly illustrated magazine, which members get for free; members also get access to the club's library. He can also use all the 500 cottages enlisted with the club. Not just in Czechoslovakia: he is entitled to lodging and food in the cottages in Poland, Yugoslavia and Bulgaria as well, at a very low cost. All for two rupees! In addition, if a member meets with an accident during his travels and loses use of his limbs, the insurance company of the club will pay him one rupee every day for the rest of his life. In the event of his death, the member's next of kin will get one thousand rupees. It's all taken care of.

Without further ado, I paid my two rupees, got my card and showed it to my friend.

Mirek said, 'Now we have to buy a rucksack for you.'

'Why? Why do I need to get one?' I asked.

'Otherwise how else will you carry your things while you're walking?'

'We'll not be carrying anything with us when we're walking.'

'There are places where there are no trains, no buses. There, we will have to carry some of our things with us.'

'We'll hire a porter in such places.'

With a mischievous smile on his face, Mirek said, 'Okay, we'll hire a porter where possible. But we shall still need a rucksack. It will come in handy, you'll see.'

Little did I know then that porters are scarce in Europe. Not just scarce, they're simply not available except in major railway stations. If I'd known that earlier, perhaps I would have sneaked out of Prague.

We bought rucksacks and, in addition, a spirit stove, some light utensils, a water flask and a strong, rugged pair of boots to climb the mountains. We felt very happy with our purchases, and looked forward to the days we would be spending picnicking in the woods, next to streams, sitting on the side of roads—what could be a more enjoyable way of spending our vacation than this?

Thanks to our Tourist Club cards, Mirek purchased two train tickets at a big discount. On his return, he said, 'I saw a large, colourful poster while buying our tickets. There's a big exhibition going on at Uherské Hradiště. It's our national fair and as it is, the place is on our way. You absolutely must visit it!'

Though I was a little taken aback by the difficult name of the town, I had to put on a brave face. 'That's really wonderful! I'd really like to go there. What should we see at the exhibition?'

Mirek said, 'You must have heard of the regional costumes of our villagers. They are very colourful and beautifully embroidered; each village has its own costume. At this fair, villagers come in their traditional dresses. Day after tomorrow, they will display their local costumes, folk songs and folk dances. This is a great opportunity. You should see for yourself the beauty and colours of the people of South

Moravia. How colourful their clothes and how vibrant and joyful their lives! You can tell your folks back home about this when you go back.'

I said, 'Certainly. If it's really memorable and touches my heart, I shall certainly tell my people about this. Give me my ticket, and I'll meet you at the station tomorrow.'

Next morning, we were on our way to Uherské Hradiště. We opened the map of Czechoslovakia we'd obtained from the Tourist Club; the cottages of the club were marked on the map. We found the cottage at Uherské Hradiště and found a little asterisk next to the spot, with the words 'This cottage is open only for the summer months of June, July and August. It is closed for the rest of the year.'

What sort of a tourist cottage was this? I thought to myself, and Mirek too was quite surprised.

He said, 'Let's get there first, then we'll find out.'

FOUR

On reaching Uherské Hradiště, we located the Tourist Club cottage without any difficulty. It was no cottage—it was a school! Thanks to the three-month summer holidays, the school was closed.

The mystery was solved. During the three-month summer break, the tourist cottage was available. For those months, tourists spent their nights in the small building; for the rest of the year, the village children learnt their alphabets and their sums in its rooms.

The place was packed with travellers. The manageress scratched her head when we requested for a room. 'There's no place whatsoever, not even an inch. Everybody has come for the exhibition, as you can see. People had written to us months in advance making their reservations. You have come here unannounced. How do I find place for you?'

We looked really worried and disappointed. 'What do we do now?'

The manageress looked equally worried. 'Right now, you will not be able to find any vacant room in any hotel or even in anybody's house. They are all completely occupied.'

We were heartbroken. 'Nothing at all? Do we have to go back then?'

'There is only one thing that I might be able to do, in case you agree to it,' she said. 'Upstairs, at the corner of the terrace, there's some space available, and I can get someone to spread some hay for you. I hope you can spend the night on a bed of hay; many latecomers like you are staying overnight like that.'

'Certainly!' we said, relieved. We left our bags, signed up in the register and ventured out looking for something to eat.

At the dining table, Mirek asked, 'Do you have a sleeping bag?'

'What's that?' I asked.

'Nothing very much, but it's very handy if you need to spend the night in odd places...like tonight. How will you be sleeping on hay without a sleeping bag?'

'What is it anyway?'

'Exactly what it says. Just a large cloth bag. When you want to turn in for the night, you just get inside the bag. So, no dirty hay, dirty bed clothes, dirty pillows, dirty blankets, none of these things will touch you. If you don't have one, buy one quickly.'

Immediately after dinner, I went out and bought a sleeping bag.

The fair had opened officially, but the peasants were still to come. So, we decided to take this opportunity to visit a typical local village. About five miles from Hradiště, there is a small village called Vlčnov, famous for the fine needlework on their local costumes. We really wanted to see the villagers at their homes, so we decided to visit Vlčnov and return to Hradiště in the evening.

At the bus station, we discovered that there was no bus to Vlčnov. Disappointed, we were about to turn back, when Mirek had a bright idea. 'So what if there's no bus? Let's walk.'

Walk five miles! I was quite dismayed, but didn't want to show it. I made a brave face and asked, 'Good idea! We can walk up to there, but how do we come back?'

'We walk back.'

'How's that possible? How can a man walk 10 miles?'

Mirek was reassuring. 'We'll certainly find a cart on our way back; many carts come back this way carrying straw and hay at dusk.'

Thus encouraged, we started on our foot journey. The road was through fields of grain, getting ready for the harvest season. Beautiful it certainly was, but walking on the village road in the heat of the sun was quite difficult for us, untrained in the art of walking. We were desperately praying for a cart on the way back, otherwise walking all the way would be really fatiguing. Looking around us, we couldn't find a single cart or bale of hay or a load of straw in any direction as far as we could see. Surely, there was suffering in store for us on the way back!

Vlčnov is a very small village, what we'd call a hamlet, but extremely pretty, and the residents very hospitable, welcoming us gladly into their hearts. We met a peasant couple who refused to let us return to Hradiště that evening. 'We know you'll be uncomfortable in our little cottage. But you must stay over one night and see how we lead our lives.'

This was an invitation we just couldn't refuse. During my entire stay in Europe, the thought that I could possibly spend a night with a villager's family in Southern Moravia had never even crossed my mind. We gladly accepted their hospitality. What helped was the thought that we would not have to walk all the way back to Hradiště and then try to sleep on a bed of hay spread on the floor.

The home of Farmer Soban was a clean and tidy cottage consisting of a few rooms, around a courtyard with a duckhouse. Across the yard were the stables—in this part of the world, they used horses rather than oxen or bullocks to plough their fields. Behind the stables was a little garden, with apple trees laden with fruit. In this garden, Madam Sobanova spread out a mat for us, and brought us a large bowl of honey, fresh from the hives and some lovely, thick local bread. This was the true hospitality of the peasants of Southern Moravia.

We fed ourselves to repletion and had a long nap under the shade of an apple tree.

Soban woke us up. 'We're going to collect hay and straw from the fields.'

'Now? Why?' I asked.

Mirek explained, 'At this time of the year, there's not much work for the farmers, since the crop is not yet ready for harvesting. They are now busy collecting husk, bits of grass, hay and straw and storing them in their barns. When winter comes, and no grass grows in the frozen ground, and all the trees have shed their leaves, these bits of hay and straw is food for the horses and other animals. All over Europe, in early summer, you'll see the same sight. In every field, you will see stray and hay being gathered, cut, bound into bales and loaded onto carts, which return home in the evenings, filling the road, the village and the fields with the sweet smell of newly mown hay. Until this wonderful redolence wafts past your nostrils, it won't even feel like summer.'

'Then, let's go and join them in their task of cutting hay and grass!' I was quite excited.

We found ourselves in a field of clover, where the plants were half as high as us, the flowers waving and heaving in the breeze. Standing in the middle was Soban, who gave me a huge scythe and said, 'I believe you wanted to join us in cutting grass. Here you go!'

I rolled up my sleeves, lifted the scythe and took a swipe at the roots of the clover plants. Nothing happened—the plants simply leaned to one side and straightened themselves up in the next moment. I tried again and again, but I never could get the hang of using those huge and heavy scythes, with their four-feet-long blades. This was getting embarrassing. I was wondering how to get out of this with my head held high, when Soban's small son saved me from shame. He had been playing at some distance away. Suddenly, he straightened up with a big smile and ran towards us, eagerly clutching something in his hand.

When he came closer, we saw that he was holding a bunch of clover leaves. The farmer's wife, Mrs Sobanova, was very excited.

Clover leaves

'See what my son has got! A five-leaved clover! Come and see!'

The clamour and the excitement convinced me that they had all gone mad! My friend said, 'It's not madness. A typical clover has three leaves on one stalk. Finding a four-leaved clover is supposed to be the sign of good luck. If you find a five-leaved clover, then you're a king, my friend!'

'Is that it? I shall find a five-leaved clover just now, just you wait and see.' I dropped my scythe, quite happily I might add, and started searching for the promised clover. But I was dogged by bad luck. Searched as I might, I could not find a four-leaved clover, let alone a five-leaved one. Not that I was really disappointed—the relief of getting rid of the scythe was considerable enough.

Soban's cart was filled up with clover; the load was about as high as a man. We yoked horse to the carts, sat down on the piles of clover and hay, and returned to the village smelling sweetly of freshly cut hay and straw. I have spent very few such happy, contented days in Europe.

Beep! Beep!! Beep! Beep!!

The blare of car horns woke us up the next morning. We looked out of the windows and saw that two buses were standing outside the cottage and blowing their horns incessantly, only for us. All the village boys and girls were already in the buses which were headed to the fair at Hradiště, and they wanted to take us with them. There was no question of any further sleep. We jumped out of bed and rushed to get ready.

Mrs Sobanova brought us two cups of coffee and told us

to hurry. The kids were running out of patience.

'What about you? Aren't you coming too?' we asked.

'We can't go now, there's so much to do! Let the youngsters go now; we'll join you in the afternoon.'

We got into the bus. Everybody was dressed in the local costume of Vlčnov, which was very pretty, flawlessly embroidered and decorated. My London suit of coat and trousers looked really uncouth amidst such colour and beauty.

As soon as the bus left, the boys and girls started singing Moravian folk songs. One song after another, each more beautiful than the previous. We had no idea when and how we finally arrived at Hradiště.

A village boy in traditional dress with his favourite companion

A procession was to go out on the main thoroughfare of Hradiště. The youngsters from Vlčnov went to find out the details of the procession, while we returned to our school house to explain to the manageress as to why we did not return the previous night.

Next stop, the main road of Hradiště. From one end to the other, the procession would go, and finally all the participants would gather in a huge field at one end of the road, where the folk festival was to take place, showing off the songs, dresses, dances, traditions and customs of the various villages that were taking part.

We chose a central spot from where we could see the processions from different villages, and also the songs, dances and enactments of rituals and customs of the participants. One group after another, the villagers came in an unending stream, dancing and singing and twirling, boys and girls together. Each village had its own unique costume, and its own unique music.

Farmer's wife in Southern Moravia decorating her home before a local festival

What a wondrous scene! What enormous energy! Boys were singing and dancing, girls were not to be left behind, singing and dancing with equal gusto. From both sides of the road, spectators cheered and encouraged the participants, throwing paper flowers at them.

One group went past, and we could hear the songs of the next group, and immediately the spectators would start tapping their feet to the new rhythm and swaying to the new beat. And so it continued—like an endless river, which sweeps us away to new heights of excitement and pleasure.

I wondered where all these village boys and girls came from.

When the last group went past, we were dizzy and bedazzled. With all the spectators, we ran to take a good position on the field where all the participants had gathered.

All the spectators were guided to the viewing areas around the field. Most of the spectators had to stand. There was a small gallery for those who had bought tickets; there were a few dignitaries and other invitees who had the privilege to sit in the gallery without tickets.

My friend and I did not belong to the category of dignitaries and invitees. And we didn't want to buy tickets either. So we stood with the others to watch the folk festival.

The festival went on all afternoon. The customs and traditions of different seasons; rites for different occasions; wedding dances, customs and festivals; harvesting rites and dances; bringing the harvest home; the rites of cutting wood in the forests; getting rid of ghosts and driving away bad luck—the variety of enactments of various customs was almost endless.

The boys and girls were unstoppable, their energy boundless. When the festival came to an end at dusk and the spectators broke up and went their separate ways, we could see small groups of boys and girls still singing and dancing in the inns of the town.

I can say this in all honesty: of all the costumes from different villages that I saw that day, the finest and the prettiest of them were from the village of Vlčnov.

FIVE

At nightfall, after an entire day spent out of doors watching the folk festival, we dragged our tired bodies to the school house, slipped inside our sleeping bags and slept the sleep of the innocent.

We woke up well into the next morning and started to get ready for the next part of our journey. Next stop: Slovakia.

Slovakia is a mountainous region, and the chief mountains are the Tatra range. On one side of the range is Poland, and on the southern side is the Lower Tatra range. At the foothills of the Lower Tatras is a village called Mýto—our next destination.

We got down from the train at a station, and had to catch a bus to Mýto from there. This was the last station on the line, and just before disembarking, Mirek brought out his rucksack and started to pack it; he also told me to bring out only the essentials that I would need and pack these into the rucksack, because from now on, we would be travelling with our rucksacks. Mirek taught me how to pack the rucksack properly, so that I could easily reach for the things that I wanted, and at the same time, not mess up all my clothes and other contents and spoil the order of things inside.

I thought this was a good idea. While climbing, we

would use our rucksacks; all our other belongings could go with us from place to place, and where required, we could hire porters. As for the heavier things, we could have them shipped from one place to another by rail or by post.

However, when we got down at the station, Mirek shipped all our boxes by rail to Prague. I was so taken aback that I couldn't even open my mouth to prevent him from doing so.

When the train left the station with our boxes and other baggage, I had recovered enough to argue with Mirek about the wisdom of this act. 'That was not a clever thing to do! Suppose we need something or the other from the stuff you've packed off to Prague?'

Mirek said, 'We are now vagabonds, a pair of tramps! We are going to walk from now on, and we must be light enough to do so without effort.'

'So, we shall walk as we please. But at night, we'll have to get back to our cottages, right? Suppose we need some odds and ends at that time, then what happens? You've already sent most of our belongings off! We have no formal clothing in our rucksacks, not even a decent tie!'

Mirek replied, 'Don't worry about it. Now we are proper vagabonds, without any ties with home. We shall move like gypsies, from one place to another, on our own two feet. We shall spend our nights at the tourist cottages. We shall not need formal clothes nor ties.'

I liked such talk, but I was still tied to my bags, now vanished in the direction of Prague. 'Okay, I understand. But since we will be using porters, we could have a couple of porters more for our boxes.'

Mirek started laughing. 'Porters? What porters? Is this a rail terminus or a port that you're going to hire porters? No porters. We're going up the mountains!'

No porters! Good grief! I thought to myself.

I still was arguing the point when we boarded our bus. 'Well, porters are not available. But we could hire horses or ponies or mules on our journey. Look at my country...people travel from Darjeeling or Kalimpong to Tibet and use mules and horses to carry their baggage.'

Mirek smiled. 'No, Sir! Here, you won't find horses or mules in our mountains. You carry whatever you need on your own shoulders.'

Somewhat dejected, I thought about my plight. When I pulled my rucksack onto the bus, it felt really heavy. The very thought that I would have to carry it on my shoulders from now on was depressing. I asked Mirek, 'I have a second pair of boots in my rucksack. Do we really need that? Can I not get rid of it? Surely the one pair I'm wearing should be good enough.'

I was so desperate to reduce the weight of my rucksack that I was prepared to throw a brand new pair of boots.

Mirek said, 'Boots are our most valuable possessions from now on. You can't throw them away!'

I sighed and with a heavy heart, stared at my rucksack and did a quick but thorough mental calculation of all the things I had packed. Is there anything there which I could dispense with? Sadly, I came to the conclusion that every single thing in the bag was really essential and just could not be thrown away.

We reached Mýto, sitting at the foot of the hills, with a tiny brook burbling away through the town. Mýto is surrounded on three sides by mountains, of which the highest is on the northern side of the town. Right now, it was covered by dark-blue clouds.

My friend pointed at the clouds and said that's where we would have to go. 'The Tourist Club has a cottage right there.'

Mirek's words had me slightly worried. Does he want us to shoulder our rucksacks right now and start climbing towards the cottage? Hurriedly, I said, 'See how beautiful this village is, nestled at the bottom of the valley! Look at this pretty little brook, and this lovely little road wending its way along its bank! I'd really love to spend a few days here.'

'That's a good idea,' Mirek said. 'The clouds will also have gone away by that time. Otherwise, it'll be really sad if we climb the mountain and find only clouds and rain. Also, we shall have a day to buy some foodstuff to take up with us.'

I shouldered my rucksack. Quite heavy, I thought to myself. If we had to add more food to the pack, I won't be able to lift it at all, I thought. 'Let's find a place to stay,' I told Mirek. 'We can think of our stomachs later.'

Finding a place to stay was easy. Mirek got very busy getting things ready for our journey ahead. We bought two huge loaves of hard, solid bread, butter, cheese, and a couple of dozen eggs. We filled up our spirit flasks. In addition, we bought a couple of pounds of potatoes, another couple of pounds of apples and about a pound of oranges.

'Why do we need all this?' I wailed.

Mirek paid no attention to my wails. He divided all this

into two equal parts and loaded our rucksacks. I resolved that from the next day I should start to eat as much as I could of the apples, oranges and bread, so that I could reduce the weight of my rucksack.

SIX

Quack! Quack!

We woke up suddenly; it was morning already. Peering out of the window, we saw a brace of ducks waddling their merry way down through the village road to the river. The golden morning sun shone on their wing feathers. The blue skies of Slovakia was awash with the delicious colours of bright sunlight, which flowed down the hills around the village and finally into the village. This was the kind of sunshine that drew people out of their homes in this land; this was the kind of sunshine that made people gather around in groups and wander through fields and meadows, riverbanks, woods and forests—the kind of sunshine that opened up the tap of gladness in every heart.

This very same sunshine came to Mýto village on this day and dragged us out as well.

Mirek would not stay indoors for another second. 'We'll never get a more wonderful day to begin our journey. We're leaving now,' he said.

You would really want to walk in the lanes and paths of this beautiful mountainous land on such a beautiful, sunny day. I also wanted to get out of our cottage and take to the road, and particularly, enjoy a picnic on a little glade next to the forests. But the very thought of carrying that enormous rucksack up the hilly roads was a real killjoy; I was convinced that I would have to return without reaching even a quarter of the way up.

However, there was no escape. I brought out an apple from the rucksack and took a pensive bite. Tea had been served, and Mirek picked up a cup and exclaimed, 'What's the matter with you? The bright sunlight seems to have cast a shadow on you. Aren't you feeling happy?'

'I feel a little sad at the thought of leaving this beautiful little village,' I said.

'Once you reach the top of the hills, you'll forget all about this village. Now, finish off your apple quickly and let's go,' Mirek replied.

I'd finished my apple, and had started on an orange. 'What are you up to? If you eat so much, how will you climb?' asked Mirek.

'Trying to reduce the load,' I confessed.

Mirek closed the top of my rucksack and tied it off with a strong rope. 'There! You won't get any more oranges once you start up the mountain; preserve what you have in your bag.'

Knowing the futility of further arguments, I got up. The rucksack settled down like a weight on my shoulders and back. I felt I could walk a little bit with this weight. I decided to walk till the forest, out of sight of the villagers, and have an honest heart to heart chat with Mirek. 'Listen, Mirek,' I was going to tell him, 'I'm the son of gentlefolk, I've never had to carry weights like a porter; carrying this rucksack around is beyond my modest abilities.'

Peasant lads were taking all the village cows to the eastern part of the village. Grass-cutters had started cutting grass on the slopes of the hills. Woodcutters were wending their circuitous way up the mountain towards the forest. Behind them came the village lasses carrying baskets to pick wild berries.

We watched all these snippets of village life while walking northwards up the highway. Mirek took a look at the map, on which was marked the footpath that we were to take from Mýto to the Ďumbier cottage, up in the mountains.

Wild strawberries

Mirek showed me the map. 'You see this path marked in red? This one, that winds its way up the mountain side? That's the path we'll have to take. Do you know why it's marked in red?'

'No,' I said.

Mirek explained, 'The roads in these hills are very confusing. You can't tell beforehand which road goes where. In many places, the roads have come together and merged into one. In many places, the road has just vanished into the grass. In some places, you can't even call it a road. In others, you think you've found a road, but it actually isn't so. It's really confusing. So much so, that at one time, you couldn't go from one part of the mountain to another without a guide. Nowadays, a system of signs has been invented which does the job of the guide. These colours indicate where the real roads exist, particularly in those places where you can easily make a mistake. A mark is painted on a rock or a tree trunk...a coloured mark on a white background. If you follow that mark, you'll stay on the road. Today, we shall have to follow these marks in red on the map.'

'I understand. But who has made all these marks? Also, how do you know if the marks have not been washed away in the rains?' I asked.

Mirek said, 'Our Tourist Club does all the markings and coding, and they ensure that these are coloured afresh every year. But, of course, sometimes they do get washed away in the rains. Sometimes, rascals wipe away the marks. It had happened in the High Tatras. A few years ago, the Tourist Club opened a beautiful cottage on top of a mountain which was difficult to climb. It was a beautiful place, so a lot of people started going there. Now, at the bottom of the mountain, there was a hotel, which started losing business, since its patrons started to climb the mountain and spend their nights in the mountaintop tourist cottage. They would, at best, have a cup of coffee or a soup at the hotel and then start their climb. The hotel owners started to remove the marks on the path to the tourist cottage. The paths in that area were quite confusing anyway; as a result, many tourists lost their way and had to come back to the hotel to spend the night.'

'Then what happened?' I was intrigued.

Mirek continued, 'I believe somebody lost his way so badly that he almost reached Poland! The Tourist Club heard of all these mishaps and took a lot of steps; they repainted the marks on all the roads, and kept some spies from among the local people. The hotel owners and staff heard about the spies and took fright. They didn't want to get arrested and be sent to jail!'

A little ahead and we found the mark we were looking for—a red mark on a white background. The mark was not showing the highway, but a small path on our left which snaked into the forest.

We followed the sign, and took the little path. Slowly but surely, the path started to climb up the slope. The deeper we went into the forest, the more frequent the red signs painted on rocks and tree trunks became. Thank God for that! If the signs were not marked out at every twist and turn of the path, we would have been in some trouble—the footpaths made by woodcutters came from various directions and merged into our path; it would not have been at all surprising if we had made a mistake and taken the wrong path.

We did not see any woodcutter, but from afar, we could hear the sound of their axes, which led us deeper and deeper into the forest. We realized one of the rules of a forest—the wood is thickest where the forest slopes gently to meet the meadow. Once we entered the forest, we were quite confused. We could not tell in which direction Mýto village was, where was Ďumbier. Only the red marks on the rocks and trees lining our winding track assured us that we were on the right path.

A small river accompanied us a little to our left; while we could not always see it, we could hear it burbling along, as if keeping time with our steps. We had been walking along for about an hour when, suddenly, Mirek ran towards the river. I ran after him without knowing the reason why. I panted, 'What's the matter?'

'Can't you see?' Mirek asked.

'What am I to see?'

'Strawberries!'

I could not see any strawberries. 'The river bank is covered with young leaves...that's all. Where are your strawberries?'

In the meantime, Mirek had taken down his rucksack and had started collecting strawberries. 'Lift the leaves, you'll find strawberries.'

I took down my rucksack. Strange, I had totally forgotten about the fact that I had been carrying a heavy rucksack on my shoulders all along. I suddenly felt very light, like a bird; I felt I couldn't stand still anymore; I had to flit, fly and dance.

'What are you doing, jumping around? You're trampling over the strawberries!' Mirek was quite annoyed by my graceless leaping around.

'I feel very light,' I said as an excuse.

'Why? Was your rucksack very heavy?' Mirek asked.

'I didn't feel as if I was carrying anything extra...it seemed to have become a part of me.'

Mirek was delighted. 'That's exactly what happens. So, now you're now an expert walker!'

'I hope you're not talking too early. We still have to climb the mountain. You'll probably find me lying on the side of the path with this weight on top of me.' I responded.

'Nothing of the sort! Now, open your rucksack and bring out your bowl and fill it up with strawberries. We can eat them for lunch with sugar.'

Thus encouraged, I also started looking for strawberries. Both banks of the river were covered with wild strawberries. The tiny berries were fresh and juicy and while picking them, I found that almost every single leaf hid a strawberry underneath. For every strawberry that I put into my bowl, I put five in my mouth. The more I picked, the more I found—it's like the berries had been hiding from a stranger like me, but once we became acquainted, they all came out to make friends with us. Soon, the river bank, which was green in colour, turned red.

Mirek brought his bowl filled with strawberries. 'You've hardly picked anything yet! Your bowl is empty!'

'I'm new at this, so it's taking a little getting used to.' I didn't want to tell him about all the strawberries I'd eaten out of sheer greed!

SEVEN

We picked up our rucksacks and resumed our trek. The climb grew steeper; we became slower. The brook became a spring and then a cascade. We were walking next to the water. The rucksack felt quite comfortable on our backs; without our rucksacks, we felt that climbing would have been more difficult.

After a while, we crossed our faithful friend, the stream, over a little wooden bridge and left her behind. Slowly, the friendly conversation of our stream became fainter and fainter. Like two brave warriors, we strode through the deeper shadows of the forest, making faint scraping noises on the bed of dry, fallen leaves on the path.

Suddenly, the canopy of leaves overhead vanished—as if by magic, and we realized that we had climbed over the forest. Right ahead, the Ďumbier mountain rose up before us, much higher than the ground we were standing on. The tourist cottage stood out like a little box on the slope of the mountain. There were no large trees on the slope, only small bushes and fresh green grass, on which sheep were grazing, looking like tiny drops of white paint.

Now the climb became a lot steeper. We were bent double under the weight of our rucksacks and swaying gently from side to side; we kept climbing in a slow rhythmic movement.

The cold air of the upper reaches of the mountain seemed to add strength to our bodies. Mirek felt so good that he sang a travel song in his native tongue. When he finished, I started to sing a favourite song of mine by Rabindranath Tagore:

চলি গো, চলি গো, যাই গো চলে।
পথের প্রদীপ জ্বলে গো গগন-তলে॥

(Choli go, choli go, jaai go chole.
Pather prodip jwale go gagon-tale.)[1]

(The pleasure of travelling, I enjoy
Lamps illuminating the eternal road.)[2]

We found another spring a little way up the road—a nice healthy spring with cool, crystal-clear water. Next to the spring was a shady glade, with rocks and bright green grass growing between the stones—it was a lovely place for a picnic. The very sight of the glade made me feel hungry.

'Mirek,' I said, 'put down your rucksack. Let's sit here for some time. Open the strings of our rucksacks and bring out our food and the strawberries.'

Mirek also liked the place, so we sat down to lunch. It was a very pretty place. On the other side of the stream was the forest we had just come through. We could clearly see the steeple of the church at Mýto. The ease with which

---

[1] http://www.geetabitan.com/lyrics/C/choli-go-choli-lyric.html, accessed 19 February 2021.
[2] Translation by Anjan Ganguly (http://www.geetabitan.com/lyrics/rs-c/choli-go-choli-english-translation.html), accessed 19 February 2021.

we climbed up such a long way from the village was quite surprising. We felt more confident. We looked at the little tourist cottage on the slope of Ďumbier and felt we would be able to get there quite easily.

Mirek started boiling the ice-cold water from the stream to make tea for us, while I started to make omelettes.

The walker's diet is supposed to be very simple, wholesome and light. However, I had been so looking forward to a rustic picnic sitting beside a mountain stream, such lovely pictures I'd painted in my mind. I remembered the many picnics I'd enjoyed at the Botanical Gardens at Sibpur, near Calcutta, and the mouth-watering menu of khichdi, mutton curry and pulao, which we put away in large quantities. I had already made quite a few omelettes and was getting ready to fry some more eggs, when Mirek suddenly noticed what I was doing and made a noisy protest. 'What are you doing? This is a feast for a glutton!'

'We have nothing else to eat,' I said.

'We have enough to eat...bread, apples, tea, plus the strawberries. How will you walk if you eat so much? Trekkers have to eat light,' Mirek told me.

How disappointing! All the visions of a feast on the lines of those we enjoyed at the Botanical Gardens instantly evaporated. We ate lightly, picked up our rucksacks and hit the road again.

The mountain path was steep. We spent an exhilarating couple of hours looking at the beautiful scenery on all sides, examining the mountain flowers and the little winding paths on the mountain. We came closer to the cottage and noticed three trekkers with rucksacks walking up the path next to the spring, like we had done, to Ďumbier. We waved at each other. We also noticed two other trekkers climbing up a little path coming from another hilltop to our right.

'The bright morning sunshine has brought so many people out on to the mountain,' Mirek remarked.

The top of Ďumbier—the highest peak of the Low Tatras—is about a thousand feet above the cottage. It had been getting foggy since the afternoon; now, it was all white. Though the sun was still shining below, by the time we reached the top, we did not expect to see anything but clouds.

EIGHT

When we reached the cottage, it was crowded with travellers from different places. Almost all 40 beds were taken. We were given two beds for ourselves. However, more travellers were expected and the manager and staff were quite worried about how to accommodate all of them. Finally, they had to make platforms and cover them with straw to make sleeping quarters.

It was pretty cold in the upper reaches of the mountain. We took out our warm coats from the rucksacks, and went to the dining hall and ordered some coffee to warm ourselves up. We also enquired about the dinner menu. The cottage provided soup and thick bread that the locals ate; in addition, one could get lamb cutlets or sausages occasionally. I took charge of the evening meal rather than risk it with my friend—the day's exertions had whet my appetite and I could eat a horse.

We were resting in the dining hall, and munching on some biscuits from our rucksacks when two persons pushed open the door. They had just descended from the peak of Ďumbier. They said that the top was completely covered in fog; nothing was visible in any direction. It had also become really cold and soon, it might even start to snow.

We quickly finished our coffees and started to climb the mountain. We felt restless and just couldn't sit in one place any more. It felt very strange to climb the mountain without our rucksacks. Not only did we feel really light, we seemed to have lost our sense of balance and if anybody pushed us, we would be able to fly.

Finally, we reached the top of Ďumbier—at a height of 6,500 feet and covered completely by clouds. Faintly through the whiteness, we could see a platform made by the Czech Tourist Club, standing tall on top of the mountain. Someone was coming down the ladder of the platform. The cold wind chilled us to the bone. We could see nothing, nothing at all, through the thickening cloud.

The person who was coming down told us, 'I've been here for quite a long time, waiting for the clouds to clear. But as you can see, the fog is only becoming thicker. It's also started snowing now. It's freezing cold.'

Little flakes of snow fell on us. The traveller was an elderly person, bent down with age, walking with the help of a large stick. We were quite surprised and said, 'You really are courageous! You've come here climbing alone at your age?'

The old man was happy to find someone to talk to. 'I really looked forward to seeing something special today. I thought that today I shall be able to see the most wonderful scenery from the top of Ďumbier. These clouds spoilt it all! Do you know after how many years I'm coming back to Ďumbier? Forty-five years. When I came here last time and climbed to the top, I was young and strong, and adventurous as well. At that time, there were no comfortable cottages to rest in, like now. The goatherds had a built a few shelters here and there, made from pieces of wood, like boxes...you couldn't call them rooms. There were no signs on the pathways. You asked directions from the villagers or you took the advice from woodcutters that you met. The rest was up to you. If you could reach the top, well done. Otherwise you went back, or you got lost and perhaps even lost your life.'

'I would never have attempted to climb up under those conditions!' I exclaimed.

The old man continued, 'I had climbed to the top at that time, taking all the trouble and risk of doing so. And it was really worth it... I felt blessed. Earth had dressed herself in gold that day. That day I realized how beautiful the light of our earth could be. I went back to the city, and grew old there; I had no connections with the mountains any more. In my old age, I reminisced a lot about my younger days, but I never thought that in my old age, I will get back the adventurous and carefree spirit of my youth. I never dreamed that I will come back to climb again. Then, my country became independent. The Tourist Club built these cottages at various places for the people of our country. It became easier to climb and to spend nights on the road. So, I took courage and left home to come here again, hoping and dreaming that I shall be able to see the Ďumbier of my younger days.'

The old man looked at us and stopped. He probably felt that we would not understand his disappointment. In a way, he was right. What would we know of or how could we appreciate the memories of events that happened 45 years ago, which he was lamenting? To us, Ďumbier was new. Of course, we would have been delighted if there was sunshine; but the bridal veil of clouds which draped the hilltop looked pretty good to us.

'Didn't you find it difficult to climb up?' I asked.

'Of course I did! On my last visit, I had got lost in the forest, finished all my food and had to spend the night sleeping under the trees, but all I felt was great happiness. This time, I suffered a lot while climbing up. I didn't mind that, but I could not see what had driven me to come up all this way, take all this trouble. That is really disappointing.'

We said, 'Why don't you stay here for a day or two? The cottage is really nice and comfortable. The sun will break out by then.'

'No. This is it for now. I will go back now and come back some other day...perhaps the sun will shine when I'm back.' The old man sighed.

When the old man left, we climbed up to the platform. Suddenly, the cloud cleared up on one side and through the clearing, we could the village of Mýto bathed in golden sunlight. But that was all—there was not the slightest clearing up of the cloud cover for the rest of the day.

When we returned to the cottage, many travellers had started brewing tea with infusers. These are very useful things for a traveller to have; if you carry one of these, you don't need kettles and other utensils for making tea. An infuser is an aluminium egg-like device with little holes all over. You fill up this egg with tea leaves, and dip it into hot water. After a while, the tea is brewed and ready.

We found that dinner would take some more time; it had become colder. So, we took out our own infusers and made tea for ourselves.

I didn't know that I had to do all my own work in the cottage. We were sitting in the dining hall for dinner to get ready, with the mouth-watering aroma of soup drifting in from the kitchen. I was feeling pretty good, looking forward to a hearty meal after eating frugally throughout the day. Thank God I had ordered the food myself and not left it to Mirek!

Mirek came in and said, 'Food's ready! Let's go and get it from the kitchen.'

'Why? We'll have to get it ourselves? They won't serve it here?'

'No. Self-service...that's the rule here.'

In Rome, do as the Romans do. So, I went and brought our food and utensils. As soon as we finished eating, Mirek picked up his plates, bowl, spoon, knife and fork and rushed off.

'Where are you going with those dirty dishes?' I asked.

'To wash them. Bring yours as well.'

'Oh. Why?'

'That's the rule here.'

The same rule applied in the bedroom as well. The cottage gave us mattresses and blankets. If required, they would give you a white sheet or a sleeping bag as well. But there are no helpful servants to make your bed. I found that everybody was making their own beds. Inexpert as I was, I had to do the same myself.

The room had about a dozen two-tiered iron bunk

beds. I climbed up an iron ladder to get to my upper deck, somehow carrying my sleeping bag, mattress, pillow, blanket and other belongings. I found making the bed quite difficult. If I stretched out my blanket, the sleeping bag went hiding somewhere; if I found and dragged out my sleeping bag, the blanket fell on the floor. I could not move about too much. A Polish gentleman was occupying the lower bunk, enjoying a mug of tea made with his infuser.

Somehow, I managed to gather all my possessions into a travelling tradesman's bundle and go to sleep.

NINE

When I woke up, most of my roommates were already up and about. Many had already packed up and were ready to start their journey. I love the warmth of lying wrapped up in my blanket, and did not really feel like getting up and getting ready. So, I turned over and went back to sleep. When I woke up again, the room was virtually empty. Mirek was up and about, shaking his blanket and bedclothes, and folding them up. He looked at me and smiled, 'That's also part of the rules here.' One more rule amongst a hundred others!

I had a wash and brush up, packed up my rucksack, made my bedclothes as per the rules of the cottage, and was ready for the day's walk. The plan for the day was to walk to the cottage at Chabenec. The journey should take six hours, with no place to halt for the night. We'd have to cross a number of mountain ridges and walk over many miles of rocky roads.

I donned my shirt and shorts, lifted my rucksack onto my back and dressed for action, I was about to start walking, when Mirek brought me up short. 'Have you changed your socks?'

I was surprised. 'Why should I change my socks now? I just started wearing them yesterday.'

Mirek said, 'That's no good! If you would like to be known as an expert walker, you must clean your feet every day and wear a clean pair of socks every day. Otherwise, the state of your feet will be quite pathetic.'

'I have just two pairs of socks. What do I do now?'

'That was a big mistake; you should have brought at least six pairs. Anyway, for now, you must wash your socks thoroughly every day, and dry them in the kitchen. When we reach a town, you can stock up there.'

After changing my socks, I truly felt like my feet had got new life. I could have walked thousands of miles right then.

On our way, we crossed a large rocky slope. Not a single thing was in green. Not a blade of grass, not a leaf, a bush or a tree was to be seen there; only a lot of cracked rocks and stones, some tinged with a thin layer of dry moss. Today, we had to follow the paths marked in blue. Some stones were marked with blue on a white background—that was the sign for our path.

It took us about an hour and a half to cross the field of stone. The merits of wearing thick and heavy boots were brought home to me. If I had insisted on wearing light shoes with thin soles, I should have had to leave them behind among the rocks.

Far away, we noticed a little shepherds' cottage, where a footpath descending downhill met our path. Three walkers were coming down that path, and we waved to each other when they were a little closer. One of them had a pair of bright green socks dangling behind his rucksack.

Mirek said, 'Hmm! Another one like you; he forgot to

bring spare socks, and where will this poor fellow dry his wet socks while he's on the road? So, there they are, hanging behind in his rucksack.'

'Yes. The rucksack is our house, our room, our verandah. It's also our courtyard where we hang out our washing to dry. We have no possessions other than our rucksack,' I retorted.

Mirek waxed philosophical. 'See how we have reduced all the weights and possessions of our lives into a few simple things.'

When we reached the shepherds' cottage, we found a few thousand sheep and three guard dogs. Inside the cottage, about 10 people were busy making cheese from sheep's milk. They spend the whole summer in the forests higher up in the mountain grazing their sheep and making cheese. Their food consist of potatoes, bread and bacon, which they bring up from the villages below, which they periodically replenish.

It was a surprise to me that these people could last for months eating such simple food. I thought of the sheep and asked, 'Of course you get a lot of sheep's milk to drink? And lamb to eat?'

'Absolutely not! Eat our sheep!? Of course we don't eat their meat, and all the milk is used to make cheese,' they said.

Making cheese was so important that they didn't eat even a small piece of the cheese they produced.

Walking on ahead, we heard the burbling sound of a spring and shortly we came upon the waterway. 'Mirek, I won't be able to move on without eating something,' I said, and without waiting for his response, I took down my rucksack.

Mirek examined the surrounding area and said, 'I think we'll get something up there. Let's climb a little further.'

'What will we get?' I asked.

Mirek said while climbing, 'Bilberries, I suspect.'

I picked up my rucksack and started climbing once more.

Shepherds making cheese

After climbing about a hundred yards, I saw that Mirek was right—there were bilberry bushes all around us.

'How did you know?' I asked.

Mirek laughed. 'The air tells me...whenever I'm near berry bushes, I get to know.'

We filled up our bowls with bilberries, just like we had done with strawberries. Bilberries are small, round, deep purple in colour and juicy. When you eat them, your tongue turns blue. You can get a lot of berries from a single bush, so it didn't take us long to fill up our bowls.

Much enthused, I started to make custard to go with the bilberries. Mirek busied himself cutting up bread, making omelettes and brewing tea. Next to the stream, two other travellers were preparing their midday meal. That's the custom of travellers: find a mountain stream in the afternoon, put down your load and prepare your meal.

We rested for a while and then packed up and went on our way. We still had a long way to go. We followed the blue signs, crossed the stream and forests, and walked ahead. The road did not seem to end. There were no signs of any village or even a homestead. We cross one mountain slope with the hope that round the next corner we shall see the cottage at Chabenec. But all we encountered were forests and hills, hills and streams, streams and forests. The load on my shoulder felt very heavy. 'Let's drink some tea and get some strength. What do you say?' I asked Mirek.

Mirek encouraged me to move on. 'Come on, let's get walking. We'll eat when we reach the cottage, not before that. Now let's move.'

The sun had set. During summer in Europe, dusk lasts for quite a few hours even after sunset, and darkness descends slowly and gradually. But darkness of the evening was coming closer and was not too far away. Our tired bodies, tired minds and tired legs did not want to move even one more step. When we had just about given up hope of reaching the cottage in daylight, we suddenly noticed it, nestled in the lap of a naked mountain slope. A thin blue strand of smoke was going straight up in the air from its chimney.

All our exhaustion evaporated instantly. We found renewed strength in our bodies and feet. This cottage had been our destination; this is what we'd been searching for all day. Finding this cottage at the end of our day's journey filled us with such joy—it is difficult to explain this exhilaration to those who have not experienced this. We raced to the cottage with wings on our feet.

After being out in the cold and wilderness, the warmth and the company of the walkers assembled at the cottage were really welcome and brought new life to us. This cottage was smaller than the earlier one, and there were less people staying over, but it was situated in more picturesque surroundings.

We ate some food and our exhaustion vanished miraculously. A group of travellers had gathered around a large map of the area and were planning their way ahead. It was a beautiful large-scale map of the Lower Tatra region, which gave many details such as the height of each place. It also showed paths, forests, streams and other landmarks.

The last couple of days had shown me the joys of

examining a map. All the forests we had walked through, all the slopes we had climbed so slowly, like a pair of snails, all the streams we had crossed and will be crossing in the next few days, all the hills and valleys we would cross tomorrow—all these were indicated in the map like little tales. A glance at the map and we could imagine ourselves walking through the forests, and crossing the streams and hills on our onward journey the next day.

Trekkers on the High Tatras

We looked at the map for our next destination, a place called Koritnica. This habitation was built around a number of hot springs, known as 'spas', which attracted many people since the waters were known to help cure or manage many illnesses. The map showed that there were two routes to get to the spas. One was through some pine forests along the slope of the mountain; the other wound almost all its way along the spine of the mountain range. We had walked through forests and along slopes, but never along spines of ranges. So, we chose the second route and were quite excited at the prospect of seeing valleys on both sides of the hills during our walk next day.

TEN

I woke up early in the morning and went to the kitchen to get some warm water to shave; the socks that I'd washed at night and put out to dry next to the hot stove had dried up quite well indeed. Of course, I had to wash my socks very reluctantly—after all who wants to do that tedious chore after a long, hard day of walking? But my friend was really stubborn. In the evening, he took out some washing powder from his rucksack and handed it to me, and I knew there was no way I would be spared. I had to become a washerman. I also learned that there was nothing that could not make its miraculous appearance from the innards of the rucksack of an experienced trekker.

Our destination for the day was Koritnica. We started climbing and reached the top of the hill as soon as we could. From then on, we walked along the spine of the range. During our entire trip, that was the most beautiful path that we had taken. It was like walking in heaven. The earth seemed below us, with its water, land and dust. For miles and miles, we walked along one spine till we reached the end of one range, and then we took another path on the spine of another range. We walked for hour after tireless hour.

Towards the afternoon, I felt tired and hungry. Mirek

also agreed that we needed to eat and rest a bit. 'Where will we get water? I haven't seen a single stream or spring so far,' he said.

I said, 'We won't find any spring on top of hills, so let's go downhill for some distance.'

Mirek agreed. But we couldn't agree on which direction to take while going downhill. Quite a distance downhill, there was a dense pine forest, where we would most likely find water, but there was no path going down there. We didn't want to go downhill aimlessly. We weren't sure that we would find the same way back, and of course, there was a chance that we might get lost. Further, we had no idea how far we would have to go to find a spring or a stream.

We discussed this for a while and finally agreed that we would not deviate from the paths marked on the map and on the ground. We hoped that there would be sources of water on these paths—otherwise, how would people be able to walk for seven or eight hours without the precious liquid?

We walked ahead on the path, and around midday, we found a group of trekkers coming towards us; they would surely be able to tell us where we could find water.

Before we could speak, they asked, 'Friends, did you see any spring or stream from where you are coming? We're dying of thirst!'

'Spring or stream? We've been walking for about four hours, and we haven't seen any source of water on our way. In fact, we were about to ask you about how much longer we'd have to walk ahead to find some water.'

They were not encouraging. 'Then we're in trouble! Look

at our state! We haven't found any water at all. You'll have to walk almost till you reach Koritnica, and you'll find a spring about a mile before you reach the village. That's another three hours away, if you walk fast.'

There was no time to lose in small talk, since both groups were in the same state. We walked on and I told Mirek, 'Let's forget about looking for water and eat some of our sandwiches. Thank God we had brought some oranges with us!'

Mirek smiled. 'See! I had told you that you would realize the value of those oranges up in the mountains!'

We sat on the barren hilltop, devoid of any grass, bush or tree, and ate our luncheon of cheese sandwich and oranges. The oranges just about managed to quench our thirst for us to stride ahead. After about an hour of such energetic progress, we felt really thirsty and I was tempted to bring out my last orange from the rucksack, when I noticed many bilberry bushes on the hillside.

Wonderful! We almost threw down our rucksacks and rushed to the bushes. These berries were slightly larger than the ordinary bilberries and a little lighter in colour as well—perhaps due to the fact that these were growing at a higher altitude.

We tasted a few berries; they were extremely juicy but were not as sweet as the bilberries we had eaten earlier. I looked at Mirek, he looked equally disappointed. We tried a few more—no, they were not as tasty as bilberries.

Mirek saw a farmer walking along the path and asked him, 'What berries are these? They don't taste as good.'

The farmer looked at the berries with distaste. 'Why are you eating those? They are poisonous.' Without another look at us, he walked away.

We were stunned. What do we do now? Where did the farmer go? He had vanished, just as he had appeared from nowhere, like an evil spirit of the woods! We stuck our fingers down our throats and tried to bring up the berries we'd swallowed. We'd not drunk any water. Our throats were dry, so we did not succeed in throwing up.

We picked up our rucksacks and hurried on our way. I said, 'We have to reach some human settlement before the poison starts acting on us.'

'Of course,' he agreed.

I felt quite angry about the farmer. He just vanished! Without telling us more about the poison and its effect, how much one could eat, what were its symptoms and what were its antidotes, he simply vanished. He didn't even have the curiosity to see us suffer from the effects of the poison!

While searching for medicines in our rucksacks, we found an ounce bottle of cognac, which we'd kept in case we caught a cold and cough in the cold climate of the mountains. We took a couple of sips from the bottle, found some strength and courage, and went on our way along the hilly path.

Given the joy of walking uphill and downhill, the musical rhythm of our footsteps, the cold breeze on our skin and the beauty of the hills, in an about an hour, we had completely forgotten the fact that we had eaten those poisonous berries.

The path on the spine of the Lower Tatra range of hills started going downhill. Climbing, running and jumping down the path, we finally saw a forest of pine trees. We entered the forest. Now we shall find water, that priceless fluid which makes the pointed leaves of trees so green. It was quite cool, so we put on a coat. It seemed to us that we'd reached a green moist place after traversing a desert. We felt moisture in the air and could almost sense a mountain stream running alongside, hidden in the trees. However, we finally found the stream at four in the afternoon, when we had almost reached the bottom of the hill.

From there to Koritnica was another mile. Another path carrying the marks of the Czech Tourist Club joined our path. We realized that this one had also come from Chabenec. This was the first path marked on the map, which we had decided not to take. At the stream, we met a few trekkers who had taken this path; they told us that most travellers took this path since there were many streams on the road, so there was water aplenty. Trekkers who took the path along the spine never failed to carry water bottles with them.

The meadow along the stream was very pretty—a small field covered with velvety grass, surrounded by pine trees, upon which the golden afternoon sunlight had fallen like a weary traveller taking his rest. We lit up our stove, boiled some water for our tea and stretched ourselves on the grass. It was such a wonderful feeling! The tiresome effort of climbing up and down the mountain carrying our big rucksacks like a pair of wild buffalos; the day-long journey over stones and mud, through bushes and across fields; walking the whole day without rest and eschewing the comforts of a cottage—all these were for the sole purpose of stretching ourselves on this green grassy meadow. We looked at the blue sky and the golden sunlight and felt one with the forest and the hills.

ELEVEN

We returned to 'civilization' at Koritnica, a small spa town with all the comforts and luxuries that anybody could want. There were many doctors as well, but we didn't have to consult any since we found no reactions to our having eaten poison berries.

One of the groups we had met at the Ďumbier cottage had told us about the wonderful Demänovská Ice Cave in the Lower Tatras. They had walked from Demänovská to Ďumbier and exhorted us repeatedly to visit the ice cave.

At Koritnica, we enquired whether we could walk from there to Demänovská, and were told that the only way to get to our destination was by bus or rail. So, we decided that if we were really keen on visiting Demänovská, we would take a bus or a train.

We spent one night in the Koritnica valley surrounded by deep forests, and next day, made our way to Demänovská on the other side of the Lower Tatras.

I have never seen a cave like this. It was not man-made, but was created by a fast-flowing subterranean river. The tunnels that we explored had been carved out of rock over tens of thousands of years. The river continues to flow merrily and noisily below the lower part of the cave, just as she has done for many millennia. Sometimes she appears as a stream, sometimes a spring, sometimes a flowing river, sometimes a lake. During her journey, she has sculpted hundreds of stalactites hanging from the ceiling of the cave, and stalagmites jutting upwards from the floor. Their shapes were magical, their colours wonderful—each one a sculptural masterpiece. They had been formed over centuries by the slow dripping of water and reactions of various salts and other chemical compounds in the water and the soil of the cave.

Demänovská Ice Cave

This wonderful cave had been hidden from the curious eyes of human beings for who knows how long. One day in the dim past, somebody had gone searching for the source of a river and entered the deeply forested region of the Demänovská valley, and in this quest, found the cave. It is said that the cave was explored only about 20 years ago. Electric lights have banished the complete darkness and allow us to enjoy the gorgeous beauty of the tunnels and other parts of the cave. It's as if we have entered the realm of fairies.

We wandered around the cave for about three miles and were informed that the authorities were working on laying out electricity lines for three more miles!

About 15 of us tourists were exploring the caves with the help of a guide, when suddenly he asked, 'Do you want to know what the cave looks like without the electric lights?' and switched off the lights! And immediately, we were engulfed by blackness—a complete thick blackness which made it difficult to breathe and even to believe that we were standing on solid ground.

A few seconds of this torture was enough. We took deep breaths of relief when the guide switched the lights back on.

After coming out of the Demänovská cave, we sat down to plan our next adventure. Till a few days ago, I had thought that no long journey was possible without trains, cars, coolies and porters. After three days of walking, I was really confident that I could cover the whole world on foot!

I told Mirek, 'I have read about the Carpathian Mountains in Ruthenia, the eastern part of your country, which is deeply forested and where you can find bear, and even wolves in winter. I read that mechanized civilization has not yet entered Ruthenia and villagers still depend on farming and herding sheep for their livelihood. Let's go there for the next part of our journey.'

'Agreed!' Mirek sounded excited. 'I've always wanted to go there since my childhood. My neighbour's son had visited that region about 10 years ago, with a tent. But at that time, our Tourist Club did not have any cottages in that area. Let's see what we have today.' He opened our club's map—there were many cottages in the Carpathian region.

Examining the map, I found a place with a very interesting name—Slovenský Raj, which means 'Slovak Paradise'. This is the Garden of Eden of Slovakia and best of all, it was right on our way.

'Such a lovely name! We definitely must walk around that area,' I insisted.

Mirek agreed. 'Certainly. Slovenský Raj is a very well-known hilly region in Slovakia. Now that we have got the chance, we must see the place with our own eyes.'

We reached Spisska by train the same evening. We were to start our trek to Slovak Paradise the next day. We bought some food and other necessities, packed our rucksacks and looked forward to becoming walkers once again on the morrow.

TWELVE

The hills in the Slovakian Paradise are not very high. We had left Spisska, following the paths marked on the map for quite a long time, but there were no signs of climbing upward. For nearly three hours, we had been walking in the hot sun, quite tired and drained of energy, and frankly speaking, we were fed up of walking. We began to appreciate why trekkers preferred the hills and mountains. And then we entered a forest deep with shadows, and the path started going uphill. Suddenly, within a moment, our fatigue vanished, and we felt refreshed and rejuvenated.

Mirek started singing in time to the rhythm of our walk. We crossed mountain streams and felt the cooling mountain breeze on our faces and bodies. The very colour of the sunlight changed and became more golden. It was as if we had found our long-lost friends once again. The strain of walking in the sunlight for the last three hours vanished like a bad dream. We now understood the difference between walking in the valleys and walking in the hills.

We had just finished our midday meal sitting next to a stream when we met a group of three trekkers, who were also headed towards Kláštorisko, just like us. One of them, who was a bit of a daredevil, asked, 'Which route are you taking?'

I opened the map and pointed out, 'There's only one path...see here.'

He didn't bother looking at the map. 'No, no! There's another path. It's a more difficult route; hence, it's not marked on the map. I'm taking that route; why don't you join me? I have not been able to convince my friends to come with me...they are really timid.'

I didn't want him to think that Bengalis were also timid, so I quickly agreed.

Mirek asked, 'Is this the same path that leads to Vel'ký Sokol? I've heard of this earlier.'

'The very same,' the trekker replied. 'I know this route; I've travelled on this in the past.'

Vel'ký Sokol is a huge canyon, with cliffs going up for nearly 200 yards on both sides. At the bottom of the gorge ran a river through a narrow ravine over broken and dangerous ground. The whole area was filled with unstable broken rocks, slippery with moss that shook with every footstep, and large pine trees which had fallen from higher up the cliff walls. We had to walk very carefully along the narrow track through the undergrowth. I had the misfortune of falling and stumbling countless times while trying to navigate the path. If I had known about such travails, I would certainly have refused to take this route, without a care to the opinion about Bengalis that my fellow travellers would have formed.

We had to cross the stream many times with the help of the overhanging tree branches, all the while carrying the heavy rucksacks on our backs. In many places, we had to jump from rock to rock, and of course, in many cases, I slipped from the rocks into the river. In many places, we had to climb up and down using ladders made from blocks of wood, literally carrying our lives in our hands.

My companions had done this before and had learnt from their previous experience; I was the one who suffered. My shoes and socks were wet through and through; my hands and feet were covered with cuts and bruises and I was plastered with mud from head to toe. When I finally reached Kláštorisko, looking like an unhappy spectre, my friends consoled me: 'We've managed to cross Vel'ký Sokol; no mountain or canyon can stop us now.'

I said, 'The gorge has shown us it's magic, definitely!' [The word 'bhelki' in Bengali means 'magic, legerdemain'; I guess the pun was lost on my friends!]

Just below the peak was a huge field covered with grass, at the high end of which was the tourist cottage. When we had crossed the woods and reached the field, a villager met us. 'You can spend the night in our cottage…it won't cost you a penny.'

We looked at him in some surprise and asked him, 'Where is your cottage?'

On the lower side of the field was a beautiful spring, next to which was a straw hut. The man pointed at the hut. 'Come and take a look. You don't have to pay anything to sleep. You will just have to buy milk and bread from me. I have butter as well. I am a herder of cows and sheep in this field.'

We were quite taken with the herder and went with him to the little hut. The beds consisted of a thick bed of straw covering the entire floor—you just lay down wherever you wanted. As simple an arrangement for sleeping as could be imagined, but quite a few travellers had already taken refuge here and were enjoying their simple meal of hot milk and fresh bread. This must be the cheapest way of sleeping and eating in this country.

My friends said, 'Look at them. They are all quite poor, but look at their passion in walking around and visiting places in their country!'

After our travails of the day, none of us could summon the courage and enthusiasm to spend the night in the cottage with just a thin blanket to ward off the cold. To keep the villager happy, we bought some milk, bread and butter from him and went to the tourist cottage. We were each given a bed, beddings and blankets for the sum of half a crown per head, which worked out to three paisa in Indian currency.

Dobsina Ice Cave

We chatted with our fellow travellers who had taken shelter in the cottage. Many were headed in the direction from which we had come. One group was taking a very long route, crossing the whole of the Slovakian Paradise, and going to an ice cave called Dobšiná. This sounded really interesting. What we had seen of the Slovakian Garden of Eden today was somewhat less than heavenly. I painted tincture of iodine on my numerous cuts and bruises and told Mirek, 'Tomorrow, let's see what the rest of the Slovakian Paradise looks like.'

THIRTEEN

When I woke up in the morning, my shoes were still wet. However, that was not a deterrent. I had no shortage of socks, since I had bought quite a few pairs in Koritnica. I took out two pairs from my rucksack and put them one on top of the other, and then put on my other pair of shoes. This pair had not yet been broken in, and the way was quite long too. Hence, two pairs of socks.

The whole day we walked from one end of the Slovakian Paradise to the other; at times the journey seemed endless, but we saw nothing to match the forests of the Lower Tatras. In addition, the sight of so many people from the towns and villages of the region 'enjoying' the sights of the country made it look really crowded; it was a bit of an eyesore to be honest.

The daredevil in our small group said, 'All these towns people who come here for a day's outing and picnic, they have named this the Garden of Eden. They have not taken the trouble of walking around and enduring the pain of long journeys to see the sights of the Tatra Mountains...they've seen only their towns and this Garden. Most of them visit only those places that can be reached easily by car.'

We soon reached a good motorable road. While walking,

quite a few travellers had joined us and we'd soon become quite a crowd. On reaching the road, most of them began to feel really homesick.

Our daredevil friend winked at us. 'Now we know that they are all townsfolk.'

Most of the travellers in our group decided against going to Dobšiná and bid farewell from there. Only the three intrepid 'cavemen', who had braved the tough route of Vel'ký Sokol, took to the forest path. We found many trees bearing hazelnuts. These grow in the lower reaches of the hills. The nuts are crisp and very sweet when young. We filled our pockets with the nuts and had our fill with our tea.

It was evening when we reached the Dobšiná cave, which had closed for the night. There was no tourist cottage there, but there was a hotel where we found lodgings for the night. Next morning, we went to explore the Dobšiná cave.

We had been told that this is an ice cave. But we didn't realize that, as a result, it was going to be bitterly cold! The morning was bright, sunny and warm, so we had dressed in shorts and half-sleeved shirts. When we reached the cave's entrance, we were quite surprised to find people coming out dressed in heavy overcoats with closed collars, and vapour still coming out of their breaths and bodies. The ticket seller at the cave told us that in our clothes we should expect to freeze like large blocks of ice cream.

Perforce we had to return to our hotel and put on all the warm vests, shirts and sweaters that we had brought in our rucksacks. None of us had overcoats to ward off the cold. Looking like a weird trio of creatures, we entered the ice cave. The beauty of this cave was something to behold. The floor, the ceiling, the walls—all were made of ice. There were heaps of ice like clouds; fine glossy ice like wax and beads of ice like crystals—white, green, blue and all shades in between. Our guide told us that the cave had 4.5 million square miles of ice; it was difficult to comprehend the huge mass of ice accumulated in the cave. Walking along the tunnel, we reached a massive hall where the floor was so smooth that people went there to skate.

It was really strange to emerge from the ice cave to the green and warm world outside. We came from a world of ice into a world of emerald springtime of flowers, trees clothed in green leaves and bright sunlight. The sun had risen further in the sky and our clothing was now bothersome. We went to our hotel, got rid of our excess clothing, packed these in our rucksacks, paid our bills and took to the road again.

Which way do we go now? We could not agree. The daredevil boy in our trio hurried along to climb another peak, as if climbing peak after peak was his only goal. Our main objective was the Carpathian Mountains in Ruthenia. We ordered lunch for the two of us and studied our map. After much debate, we agreed to go to Spisska, from where we would take a train on the morrow for Ruthenia. Now the question was how to reach Spisska. We could go by car or bus. Spisska was about 40 miles away by road round the hills. The map showed us another way—a hill and on the other side was a rail station called Mlynky, from where Spisska was just a few miles. We must not ignore such an opportunity—God created such shortcuts only for walkers like us.

After lunch, we set out with our maps on the ready. We would have to rely on the map and our compass, since none of the paths in this part of the hills carried marks of the Tourist Club. That did not cause us much concern; the map showed us that we just had to go over the hill and Mlynky was right on the other side. And of course we were bound to meet other travellers on the road who would help us find the right path.

We started climbing. We came upon a circuitous path. If we stayed on this, surely we would be able to get across the hill. After a while, however, the path started going downhill. We had to abandon the path and once again rely on our compass. We found another path like the last one, and once again we were disappointed. The path insisted on going westward along the hillside, refusing to climb up.

Back to our compass. We had to leave the long grass and wade through some watery ground. Thorns had bruised our legs, so we had to change from shorts to full trousers. In all this, we suddenly realized that we had not found out the train timings from Mlynky! It was a small station and may not have many trains going through in a day. Where would we spend the night in case the last train had departed already?

With such worrisome thoughts in our minds, we hurried along and finally reached the top of the hill, where we found a pretty well-travelled footpath and a group of cowgirls. They were coming from Mlynky and showed us the route; it was about an hour's walk from where we were, and we could see the town hidden in the trees down in the valley, with smoke coming from the cottages indicating that the inhabitants were busy with their evening chores. The girls told us about the train timings. The train for Spisska would leave about three hours later, at eight o'clock. We bought some milk from the girls and made hot chocolate in our stove.

At the end of the field, the sun was setting over the line of trees of the forest. The shadows lengthened in the gloaming; the light softened and spread gently on the grass and on the souls of the men and women who had still not reached home. This is the most beautiful time of the day. During summer in this country, the sun sets taking its own sweet time over it. The light of the day fades over long hours as if it was reluctant to leave our world in the darkness to follow. In my country, all those who work in the fields would be wending their way homeward. But over here, we saw grass cutters coming up the hill from Mlynky with long scythes in their hands, going out to work. They reached some large fields covered with grass, not far from where we were sitting, and started to cut grass. One of them started singing:

Luchka zelena
Nepokosena
Di Boje ros si
Luchka sa skossi
Zaitra do rana!

(Fresh green grass covers the field,
Still uncut.
God, please give them

Your dew-filled blessings.
Tomorrow morning,
They will feel the force of the cutting blade.)

This was like a play. I loved it and turned to Mirek: 'I think I am finally seeing the real Europe.'

FOURTEEN

We reached Spisska in the evening, and I found a large number of letters—from my homeland, from London and many others from different places—waiting for me at the local post office. These had reached my bank in Prague, which had forwarded them to the Spisska post office as per my instructions. One letter was from Vienna, from my Bengali friend Satyabrata; he'd written that he had left London and cycled his way all across Germany and Austria and had finally reached Vienna. He wanted to know how I was faring and how I was enjoying my journey.

The letter took me back in time. At one point, I had also planned to travel through Europe, just like my friend, on a bicycle. I had also received many invitations for such a journey. But I did not want to travel on highways and visit large towns and cities, so I did not take up such a journey. Sure, if I had travelled on a cycle, by now I would have been to many countries and seen many large and famous cities. But, in the final analysis, what would I have gained? At that time, I did not know and so did not understand. Now I know; now I understand. Now that I am a walker, I really understand. I would have gained nothing; I would have simply wasted my time.

Satyabrata knew that I was travelling from one country to another by train. He had absolutely no idea that I was actually going on foot over hill and dale with a large rucksack on my back.

I sat down and wrote him a letter. I wrote that he had seen many sights travelling on two wheels, but if he really wanted to enjoy the hills and mountains, the villages and their inhabitants, then he must start travelling on foot and join us as a fellow trekker.

Mirek and I discussed our travel plans and felt that we should return to the High Tatras from our sojourn in Ruthenia by 19 August. Accordingly, I wrote to Satyabrata that we were going for a walking tour of the Carpathian Mountains and should come back by 19 August. If he wanted to join us, he should come to a specific town I mentioned in the letter

The High Tatras

and wait for us at the office of a specific tourist company, which I mentioned in the letter as well. We would wait for him there between 10 and 11 o'clock in the morning.

Next morning, we left Slovakia by train and travelled due east. We spent the whole day in the train and when we reached Yasinya early in the evening, all our enthusiastic expectations of visiting Ruthenia had vanished in the rain. The sky was clouded over; the very wind was moist. It had rained hard a little while ago, the roads were muddy and the whole town seemed somnolent and lacking in energy.

The Tourist Club did not have any cottages here, so we had to find a place to stay. The landlord said that it had been raining incessantly in Yasinya for the last three days and showed no indication of stopping. All the trekkers who had planned to go up the mountains were stuck in the town. Indeed some of them were even planning to go back home. The landlord told us that there was a restaurant at the other end of town which was the den of all the trekkers and travellers.

Anybody who wants to visit the Carpathian region has to come to Yasinya. You can visit all the parts of the Carpathians from here, and Yasinya in its own right is a beautiful place to visit. A lot of tourists come to see the very old and pretty wooden churches.

The restaurant was packed and lively in spite of the cold and the wet weather. A group of boys and girls were singing folk songs at the top of their voices, and the crowd was clapping enthusiastically in time. Everyone was having a wonderful time. I have never heard trekkers singing songs that were played over the radio and in films, and which were popular in the large cities. They say that folk songs were far more true to life, far closer to nature and people's lifestyle. Film songs were urban and could appeal to the sentiments of city dwellers, just like novels and plays, which were also products of urban life. But they did not touch the deepest parts of a person. Try singing film songs when you are deep in the woods, sitting on rocks, with a mountain spring burbling next to you—it will sound totally out of place.

Seeing an Indian entering the restaurant dressed like a walker must have been a surprise to all those who had gathered there. A boy and a girl came up to talk to us. From them, we learnt many things about the hills around Yasinya. They had just returned a couple of days ago from Hoverla, the highest peak of the Carpathians, covered in mud from head to toe and drenched through and through.

The paths here are quite unlike those in the Lower Tatras; here, they were covered with mud, criss-crossed with gutters and ditches, and snaked their way through thick forests of vines and old trees.

The two of them were waiting for the weather to clear so that they could go to another peak called Pop Iván (also known as Pip Iván). We made up our minds that we would visit both these two peaks: first Hoverla, and then Pop Iván.

The boy and the girl also told us that the peaks here were not like the comparatively naked peaks of the Tatras; they were totally wooded over. It was much easier to lose one's way and there were fewer villages and towns. It was absolutely important that we do not stray from the marked paths during our journey. For some reason, these two people had come to the conclusion that I had come all the way from India just to visit the Carpathian Mountains. They were so pleased at this that they expressed their happiness and gratitude over and over again. They did so in pure Czech, a language of which I did not understand a single word, and took their leave after wishing me the best of luck in my journeys.

It continued to rain in Yasinya for the next two days as well without any sign of stopping. We had already seen everything that there was to see in Yasinya. On the third day, there seemed to be a tiny break in the clouds. At the restaurant, in the evening, the talk was of making a move the next morning in case the rain held off. A forest train went from Yasinya to the mountains to bring back timber; its destination was Hoverla, so quite a few of the travellers decided to take the train. That sounded like a good idea, particularly if one wanted to avoid the rain and mud of a walk on the mountain paths. We decided to take the train as well.

We came out of the restaurant and made all the arrangements for the journey. Butter, cheese, peasants' bread, apples, lime, eggs, potatoes, sausages and spirit for fuel. Our rucksacks were filled to the brim with our purchases and became extremely heavy. In our happiness at the possibility of resuming our life as walkers, we had perhaps bought too much food.

FIFTEEN

We woke up to a beautiful sunny day that filled us with joy. We got ready in a hurry, paid our bills and ran to the little station from where the forest train to Hoverla was to depart. All the travellers who had been stuck in Yasinya for the last few days were all there—almost a hundred of them.

I'd never seen a forest department train before. It was quite funny—just a few bogies to carry goods, standing on a tiny pair of tracks, without doors, windows, tops or steps. There was no station and no platform either. We were told to get onto the train immediately and that it was going to leave right then. We flung our rucksacks into one of the bogies and jumped into it ourselves. There were no benches, so all of us stood through the entire journey.

The engine was attached to the rear of the train and everybody started to sing.

Hooyia hooiya hooiya ya
Tece voda kalna

This was the first time I saw a wood-burning engine. The noise, the smoke and the sparks were straight from hell. Now

I understood why the engine was attached to the rear of these topless carriages.

Thanks to the rains of the last few days, everything around us was wet. The soil was muddy and the water was brown and full of debris. We wondered how we would have managed to walk through such wet and muddy terrain if the rain had not stopped, when suddenly there was a lot of noise from the carriages at the front of the train. What happened?! Ah...two young men had braved the mud and wet grounds and were walking like true walkers on the forest path. 'Bravo! Bravo!!' shouted our fellow passengers. The engine driver suddenly braked hard and stopped the train. 'Come on board! Where are you going?' shouted those on the train.

'Hoverla!' answered our intrepid walkers. But they refused to board the train.

'You won't have to buy a ticket; get on the train,' assured the engine driver. But the young men would not be moved. The train started and went on its way; all of us said, 'They are true walkers!'

About half an hour later, we reached the side of the mountains. The train stopped and all those who wanted to go to the Hoverla and Pietros mountains were asked to disembark here. About 50 of us jumped off the train. The rest continued on their way to another peak called Kukul. The train would pick up timber and return to Yasinya thereafter.

There were 10 of us going to Hoverla, which was a five-hour walk, but all uphill on a wide path. The road to Pietros and Hoverla was the same for some time, and then split into two and went off in two different directions.

I espied a cottage with a cowshed, obviously the home of the forest guard, and I had an idea. I told Mirek, 'Let's see if we can get some milk there. I have some custard powder and we can make some custard pudding with our lunch.'

Mirek agreed. We told the others to carry on and that we would catch up with them soon. They took the forest path and we walked towards the cottage.

When we knocked on the door, the guard's wife came out and happily gave us some milk. Mirek asked her whether we could get some berries on the path to Hoverla. He also told her about the time when we had eaten the poisonous fruits thinking they were bilberries.

The lady told us that we could take the path through the woods behind the cottage. We should find lots of bilberry and raspberry bushes on the way.

That sounded tempting. But Mirek was hesitant. 'Where will the path through the forest lead us? We want to go to Hoverla.'

'That is the path to Hoverla. All the people in the forest department use this path to go to Hoverla and back. This is not open to public, but since you are so fond of raspberries, you can use it...we won't object.'

She took us through her garden and opened the door. 'Take this path through the woods. After walking for about an hour, you will reach the woods where the raspberries grow. From there, you'll find a path which goes downhill, it's the path the woodcutters take. There's another one which goes uphill and over the hill...take that one, and once you're over the hill, you'll see the peak of Hoverla right ahead. Just go ahead; it's straight forward...nothing to worry.'

Mirek asked, 'How far is the cottage from the peak?'

The lady answered, 'A little below the peak. You'll find a path marked with yellow paint. Take that path...one side takes you up to the peak, the other down to the cottage.'

This sounded quite simple and very reassuring. So much so that we felt that the people at Yasinya had exaggerated the difficulties of the paths in these parts. The guard's wife said, 'My two sons have gone to pick bilberries. You might run into them near the raspberry woods. If you have any doubts or questions about the path to take, ask them and they'll show the way.'

We had no further doubts. For the first time in our treks, we left the paths marked out in the map, and took an unknown route.

SIXTEEN

The steep path took us through a deep forest. We were really enjoying our walk after many days. The forests in the Carpathian Mountains were very different from the Tatras. These forests here had older, larger trees, many of which had broken down and collapsed on the paths. These woods were much larger and grander; they were wild and unkempt, more so than those in the Tatras. For the first time while travelling through Europe, I felt that I was going through forests which resembled the mountain forests in India.

After about an hour and a half, we reached a clearing, from where we could see a small part of a mountain peak standing up tall against the sky. This looked like the pictures we had seen of Hoverla. But right in front of us was another high peak, with a deep forest at its foot. We would have to cross the forest and climb over this peak in order to reach Hoverla.

Mirek broke off a branch from a nearby tree and handed it to me. 'Look,' he said.

The branch had many clumps of raspberries. I looked at Mirek. 'Can you smell out raspberries like you had claimed last time?'

Mirek said, 'Yes! Can you see the berries?'

I looked around me. We were surrounded by hundreds of raspberry bushes.

We filled out our bowls with raspberries and settled down to lunch right there, very near a stream of clear water. After a break, we started walking again, but this time, we felt quite unsure about the direction in which the path was taking us. Not only was the path fainter and narrower than before, but it seemed to be taking us downhill to the forests below the hills. However, we kept on this path in the hope that after a while it would start going uphill again. The path continued to narrow until it was just a jungle track wending its winding way downhill. The path did not look frequented. Finally, we came upon a fast-flowing mountain stream, which we crossed by jumping over the rocks in the stream. On the other side, it became really difficult to figure out which way the path went.

We put down our rucksacks and settled down on a pair of rocks to discuss our situation and decide what to do next. It was very clear that we would have to cross the mountain on the side of which we were resting if we wanted to go to Hoverla. The forest guard's wife had said that we should have to take the path going uphill after crossing the raspberry woods. But where was that path? We had taken the only path out from the woods, and that had brought us to this stream and thereafter had vanished. So, what do we do now?

The place where we were sitting was very lonely and quite dreadfully glum, surrounded completely by high mountains. In whichever direction we explored, we entered forests taking us downward which became deeper with our descent. We were getting really worried. The sun was full and we were quite tired toiling in the sunlight.

We decided that we would try one more time to see if we could find a path that is likely to take us to our destination. If we did, we would follow this path for a bit to see where it led us. But if we found that the path was taking us into the deep forests, then we'd forsake the path, and retrace our steps and go back to the guard's cottage and have it out with the good lady in the cottage. We ate a few bilberries from a nearby bush and lay down to relax for a short while.

We were cursing our greed in coming to look for raspberries, when we heard voices quite close by. A bush parted and two young men appeared in the clearing. One was about 15 or 16, with a large basket of bilberries hanging from his shoulders; his companion was a lad of some 10 summers, holding a large bowl filled to the rim with bilberries.

Mirek said, '*Dobrý den*. Good day to you. Are you the children of the forest guard?'

The older boy put down his basket and said, 'Yes. Why do you want to know?'

We described our plight in detail and told him that according to their mother, they would be our saviours if we got lost. The smaller boy said, 'You have left the path miles behind you. Come with us, we'll show you. We're taking this path to go back home.'

Mirek asked, 'How long would it take to reach Hoverla? Do you think we'd be able to reach before dark?'

The younger brother said, 'Of course, if you walk really fast and provided you don't get lost once again.'

The elder brother stopped him. 'There's another way. Why do you want to backtrack and waste your time going backwards? From here, you just climb up the side of the mountain on your left, as far as you can see. At the top of your climb, you'll find a nice wide path, which will take you to Hoverla.'

'But where is the path to climb up the mountain?' Mirek asked.

'Path? What path? Why do you need a path?' The elder brother was not impressed. 'Just go straight up, through all the bushes and small trees. There are no big trees in that direction, so just go straight up; shouldn't be a problem.'

Yes, he was his mother's son, all right! We didn't like his advice. 'We may not be able to reach Hoverla, but at least we are on pathways which people use. We are visitors, not locals, we don't know the local paths. If we get into the forests around here, we'd probably get totally lost.'

The boy said, 'Okay, then come with us. We shall reach you to the right path.'

The younger boy was not pleased at all. 'Why should we do that? It would have been a bit of a roundabout for them if they took the other path, but so what? We would have reached home more quickly. I don't feel like walking through thorny shrubs and bushes. My feet are aching. I'm going home.'

The elder brother scolded him. 'Yes, do that. And one more thing; when you talk to strangers, show them respect, be polite and always address them formally.'

We started climbing straight up the hillside. There were thorny shrubs all over; the ground had many holes hidden in the bushes and long cracks—all concealed in the tall grasses. Halfway up the hill, we stopped to rest for a while. Mirek asked the boy, 'Are there wild animals in this area?'

'Of course,' replied the boy. 'Inside the forest, you can see bears from time to time. We just saw a mother bear and her cubs in the forest we came from. The woodcutters who work in this forest all know them. Nobody bothers them, they don't bother us either, so all is well. Sometimes, you can see herds of deer with antlers. In winter, sometimes we can see wolves as well.'

Suddenly, we noticed the younger boy coming up behind us. 'I'm sorry, I behaved badly. Please accept my apologies. I hope you don't mind.'

We laughed and accepted his apologies. 'That's fine, my boy. It's all right.'

When we reached the path, our feet were bruised quite badly by thorns. Up ahead, in the distance, we could see Hoverla, another three- to four-hour walk away. The two boys put tincture of iodine on their feet and took their leave, giving us a few handfuls of bilberries as a goodbye gesture. We also put tincture of iodine on our feet and got ready to go on our way.

The day was quite hot, and the cloudy nature of the sky indicated the possibility of a storm and rain in the evening. We hurried up since we did not want to get caught in a rainstorm out in the open, on the hill. We have been walking for about two hours and crossed the line of pine trees. In front were the proud peak of Hoverla and banks of cumulus clouds in the sky.

We noticed a peasant's home on the hillside—a small cottage, a small hut with a straw thatch and a small field. We were feeling tired, and the sight of the cottage made us feel hungry as well! We walked up to the cottage; two small boys came out and Mirek asked them if they had any milk.

They answered in a language which Mirek could not understand. Neither Czech, nor Slovak; we realized that they must be pure Ruthenians. We had no choice but to resort to sign language. It worked. The boys ran to fetch us milk. We sat under the straw thatch and lit our stove and started to boil water for tea. It started raining quite heavily. Mirek was relieved. 'That was a really lucky escape!'

The two boys came back and from the way they were waving their hands, we understood that there was no milk.

We were thanking our stars that we found welcome shelter from the rain, when one of the boys placed a small bowl of solidified cream on the floor. This looked really tempting. We took out some of the bilberries that we had picked during the day. Mirek held out a handful of coins and offered these to the boys, 'How much do you want?'

The two boys picked out a few coins as payment and sold us the whole bowl of cream. The four of us sat looking out at the rain and feasted on the bilberries and cream.

When the rain stopped, the sky had cleared, with only the peak of Hoverla covered with fog. The setting sun hurried us on our way. There were many paths going off in different directions from here—some were used by people and some were merely tracks left by cattle. We took one of those and entered a forest of dwarf creeper pine trees, plentiful in this area, about the same height as a human being. The path again branched off into many forks, but none of them looked promising.

We wandered around in the forest, searching for the right path; the result was that we got ourselves literally entwined in this forest of creeper pines, completely lost and without the faintest idea of where we were and in which direction we should go. We had no time to play blind man's bluff in the forest if we wanted to reach our cottage before darkness.

We left the tangle of paths, and started climbing uphill through the trees. It was a brave journey upward through the dense forest—sometimes swinging like a pair of bats; sometimes breaking off branches; and most of the time stepping from one branch to another. Every step carried with it the possibility of our slipping off the wet branches thanks to the recent shower.

Fighting our way through the forest, we finally reached safety, achieved without a single scratch on our bodies. 'Bravo!' said Mirek. 'You seem to have completed your schooling at Vel'ký Sokol!'

We had reached just below the Hoverla peak. We walked a little further on, and found a path marked with yellow paint, put there by the Czech Tourist Club. It was like finding a long-lost friend! It was such a relief, finding the right path after spending our day wandering around lost, as if in a maze. The path on our left went up to Hoverla's peak; on our right, it went down to the tourist cottage, which we could see clearly as a tiny little house way below us.

We started to walk to the cottage, when an idea brought both of us to a stop. It was a beautiful evening. The sky was clear and gorgeous; who knows what tomorrow would be like. There was enough daylight still. Why don't we climb to the top right now?

The path went sheer up the hill. It was going to be a steep climb. We dropped off our rucksacks by the side of the path, and started going up. The sun had set by the time we reached the top. The international boundary of Czechoslovakia passed through where we were standing, marked by a series of white pillars. From there, the highest peak of the Carpathian range, we could see the valley of Rumania on one side and the valley of Poland on the other, stretching as far as the eye could see.

We had been very disappointed on reaching the top of Ďumbier, enveloped in a thick blanket of fog. Reaching the top of Hoverla was thus a wonderful compensation.

SEVENTEEN

It was getting dark by the time we reached the hilltop, so we hurried back since we had to reach the cottage before it got really dark. We picked up our rucksacks and struck out on the path marked with yellow paint, keeping a healthy pace. Looking down the hill, we saw a wide path going towards our cottage. We were quite confident of reaching this path before nightfall.

We marched on with a single-minded focus when we looked around and came to a sudden stop. The cottage was behind us! How did that happen? Where were we going? Anyway, we had to stay on this path and keep a sharp lookout for the mark of the Tourist Club. The path did not go downhill at all; it in fact wended its way hugging the side of the hill. After some distance, we saw the yellow sign of the club—that was quite a relief! So, we hadn't got lost once again after all! Now, the path would take a turn and hopefully start going downhill.

But the path continued on its way straight ahead! What was going on? This seemed to be the route to the Petros hill! The path could not be taking us to Petros, could it? That was a real possibility. The Tourist Club had a cottage there as well, but it was a long way off, a journey of a few hours.

We started getting worried. It was getting quite dark now,

and the confusion about the path was really worrying. We could see our cottage quite clearly, nestled on the hillside. To hell with all this, we thought; we'll get off the path and go directly to the cottage down the hillside, since between us and the cottage, there were very few trees. Only a handful of creeper pine bushes could be seen in the folds and crevices of the hillside, but we could very easily circumvent those on our way to the cottage. After all, we had climbed up to Hoverla the same way, and it was going to be quite a shortcut.

So, we started going rapidly downhill, skipping over stones and bushes.

We reached a forest of creeper pines. It didn't seem to be a large one, so we decided to walk around it rather than through it. But, we couldn't find any end to this 'small' forest! While trying to find a way around the forest, we got into the folds of the hillside and couldn't see our cottage any more.

That was not good. We could not afford to lose sight of our cottage, so now we decided to cut through the forest rather than walk around it and continue on our downward journey. Once we reached a clearing, we would be able to see the cottage and would have a much better idea of its location, distance and how to reach it.

So, we entered the forest of creeper pines. There were no paths in there, not even marks left by wild animals that lived there. We couldn't reach the ground in many places. The creepers had formed a huge thick net of vines and branches about three feet above the earth. We had to move forward by putting our weight gingerly on the branches below us, hanging on those above us, all the while carefully managing our heavy rucksacks so that our weights didn't send us crashing through the net of vines.

I still don't know how we crossed this pathless forest and came out unscathed on the other side after half an hour of struggle. But there was no respite—right before us was another such forest, this one about one and a half times the height of a man. We could not hope to see the cottage or even catch a glimpse of the valley. It was getting darker by the minute, and the foot of the next forest was already black. It was going to be quite unwise to enter the forest now. Since we had already come quite a lot down the hill, we must have reached close to the path to the cottage. So, we decided to walk along the side of the forest, and if we found a gap in the woods or caught a glimpse of the cottage, we would go downhill accordingly.

We reached a place filled with large boulders, cracked and jagged with sharp edges. We had to walk carefully and slowly through this place, putting one foot gingerly ahead of the other. We crossed a stream, and the boulders on the other side were even bigger, the cracks and holes sharper and even more difficult to tackle. The worst thing was that it was becoming dark really quickly now, and we could not find a single gap in the forest for us to try to go through it downhill. We had no idea about where the cottage and the path were, and how far away they were from us.

We had to go forward. It was pointless and too late to try to go back. We had left behind one forest of creeper pines, and we had no idea what was in front of us. But we had to go forward, without a doubt, as far as we could go. Every time we reached a bend in the road, our hopes soared that this time we shall find a gap in the forest, which would lead us downhill, or we shall catch a glimpse of the cottage or of the right path. But, nothing. Nothing at all. All we saw downhill was an impenetrable forest of the cursed creeper pines, and boulders up the hillside hanging menacingly above us.

The last lingering daylight had gone, and it was dark. We lit our torch—a single pencil-torch between the two of us. We pointed the light on one spot, one of us stepped into the light, and then the other one carefully followed. Like a pair of slowworms, we crawled over stones and other hurdles.

We did not give up hope. Sure we were afraid, we did not know of what—afraid of being caught in an unknown place. Afraid of being alone, just the two of us. Afraid of the complete darkness. Afraid of being without shelter. Afraid of all of these, perhaps.

Suddenly, I dropped the torch, and we immediately realized the intensity and absoluteness of the darkness through which we were struggling. But we just could not afford to lose our torch. We put down our rucksacks and brought out matchboxes. I realized that my hands were shaking. We lit many valuable matchsticks to locate our torch, and found it stuck inside a thin and deep crack. I lay down flat on the ground and reached for the torch, finally managing to get it out.

We stared at each other in the darkness. Mirek said, 'Let's call for help. Someone might hear us. I'm sure a cottage or some village or settlement is nearby.'

Both of us took a deep breath, and facing the forest,

shouted in unison, '*Pomoc*!' (meaning 'help' in the Czech language).

The darkness seemed to get even more dreadful at the sound of our voices. We shouted once more, and then once more. But there was not the slightest sound from anywhere. Underneath that black sky, standing by the silent motionless forest, our shouts sounded strange and utterly helpless. We felt that our shouts would bring us danger rather than help. We were frightened of breaking the silence of the cold, black gloom that surrounded us. We decided not to shout any more, but whisper even if we were talking to each other.

We had to spend the night in the mountains—there was no other option. We tried to give courage to each other. We had food, lots of food in fact—bread, butter and cheese. We had a stove and spirit to light it. We could brew ourselves some tea. Then we could also pick up a few branches and twigs and light us a fire; we shall spend the whole night next to the fire. Problem solved.

We found a sheltered shallow cave, with walls of stone and half a stone roof. We were at a height of about five or six thousand feet, so it had started to get cold after dusk. We brought out all our clothes from the rucksacks and started putting them on.

Then we sat down with our backs to the wall of the cave. We could relax now! The day had been exhausting. We had been looking forward to reaching our cottage in the evening, partaking of a hot dinner of pea soup and meat, and get into our warm beds for a good night's sleep. Instead, look at what we had to settle for!

The cold and our lack of warm clothing meant that we would have to stay awake the whole night in spite of how tired we were. Falling asleep meant pneumonia. We would have literally caught our death of cold. We would have to keep ourselves as warm as we could by drinking endless cups of tea.

Tea! How do we get the water to make tea? We didn't have a single drop left with us any more. We had crossed a stream a short distance away, but it was impossible to go back and find it in the darkness. We had to say goodbye to tea. We were famished. We brought out whatever food we had in the rucksacks and started eating. We were pretty thirsty as well, but we had to make do, for now, with just half an orange each.

We went into the forest with our torch searching for dry wood. The forest had been drenched in the rains of the last few days and everything was wet. We scrounged a few handfuls which were somewhat dry and piled them on the stones in front of our shelter. I had a Bengali newspaper in my rucksack, which I read from time to time. I tore out

Outdoor cooking and tasting the food

one sheet after another and tried to set the pile of wood on fire. It didn't work. We wasted a lot of paper and a lot of matchsticks before we realized that we won't be able to set this pile of wood on fire. We still tried to blow the tiny flame of our matchsticks into setting the pile on fire, but more as a matter of play—this might help us while away the long hours of the night, we thought.

We reluctantly had to call a halt to this when our stock of matchsticks dwindled alarmingly. Sitting bundled up on the rocks was difficult. If we didn't keep ourselves busy, we'd fall asleep. And it was getting really cold now. Suddenly, I remembered that we had some cognac in a flask tucked away in one of the pockets of my rucksack. We had a spoonful each. It turned out to be a great antidote to the cold. We calculated that we had enough cognac to last us through the night, if we rationed ourselves to one spoonful each every hour till daybreak.

'Instead of keeping quiet, let's tell stories by turns,' I suggested. 'Whoever is falling asleep will start. But it has to be really funny stories. Horror stories not allowed!'

Mirek accepted my suggestion and the storytelling session went on successfully for quite a while.

Our battle against sleep took most of our energies. Our bodies were really tired; if we had rested our heads on the bare rock, we would have gone off to sleep instantly. We dozed off while listening to each other's stories; our words got slurred while telling them.

Somehow, in this fashion, we managed to stick it out till midnight. With half the night over, we felt that we had got over the worst as far as sleep is concerned. But it seemed to get a lot colder. We went a little deeper into the shallow cave, huddled closer to each other and had another spoonful of cognac each.

We looked out at the blackness and saw the most beautiful night sky that I have ever seen. The sky was no longer inky black; it had a strange but lovely hue. There was no moon. There were countless stars in the sky, but the hue was not from the starlight. I was told later that light in the mountains is like that. Sitting in the dark night, beside the gloomy forest, on the bitterly cold mountain peak, surrounded by complete silence, we were really unnerved and, to be honest, quite scared—as if something was waiting to pounce on us, hidden in the darkness.

But we didn't let on, even to each other, that we were scared. On the contrary, we tried to give each other courage. We told stories—all the funny and not-so-funny things that have happened to us were told and retold with wild exaggerations and extrapolations, trying to make each story last for as long as we could. After every story, we looked at our watches.

It was now three o'clock. For the last hour or so, we'd been noticing that a bank of clouds had climbed from behind the mountain peak and had slowly spread itself to cover the whole sky. All the stars were now hidden and the sky was even darker now, if that was possible. Suddenly, the whole sky was split by a bolt of lightning. The sound of thunder assaulted our ears. The cloud bank was now in wild disarray.

We realized that our night of suffering was far from over.

It was soon half past three in the morning, and the first light of the morning was trying in vain to peep through the stormy clouds on the horizon. And then it started to pour.

We put on our raincoats and tried to shelter ourselves as best as we could in the little cave that was our refuge. But from our waist down, we were totally drenched. We couldn't save our rucksacks either from the same fate. After half an hour, our necks and backs were in agony, when the rain stopped just as suddenly as it had started. The first light of dawn very gingerly lit up the horizon. We wrung out the water from our socks, put the rucksacks onto our reluctant backs and resumed our journey to the cottage.

There was no way downhill. The dense wood of creeper pines stood staunchly in our way. We had a long walk the previous night along the edge of the forest; how much longer we would have to walk this morning, only time would tell.

We decided that we would no longer walk blindly, as we had done last night. It would be wiser to climb upward until we could see something—either the tourist cottage or some sign of habitation, or a person or a path. As decided, we went up the hill, and after a while, felt warmed up from our exertions.

We halted in a clearing and looked around. The forest of creeper pines went on and on for as far as we could see. However, there appeared to be a gap in a line of tall pine trees, which we managed to reach after some tricky climbing.

Some carpenters had worked there recently and had left a little footpath going down the hill. But we could not see any road, path or cottage from here. Anyway, we started walking downhill along the footpath and after a while, lo and behold, we entered yet another forest of creeper pines! We could express our anger and disappointment only with the choicest invective. Was there no escape for us from creeper pines?

'What do we do now?' asked Mirek.

'Since there is a pathway, let's follow that through this forest,' I said.

The forest became more and more dense, and the path grew narrower and thinner. At one place, it looked like a herd of deer had gone along the path just a few minutes ago. As we went ahead, the tracks became more frequent, deeper and clearer on the wet footpath. It was obvious that there was a stream or a spring close at hand, and the footprints indicated that the herd had gone uphill along this path after the rainfall.

Suddenly, we were stopped in our tracks by a loud continuous noise, which shook the forest—it was the call of the wild deer. We turned around and beheld a sight that we shall never forget: a long line of deer walking along the side of the hill, very close to where we were standing, casting their shadow on the hillside in the early morning sunlight. It was an indelible picture which more than made up for all our trials and tribulations of the previous night.

We followed the deer track along the footpath and soon reached a spring, and lurking close by, we found the wide path we had been looking for, which had been hiding from us last night. We stepped onto this path, and carefully started to climb downhill towards our goal. It seemed like we stepped into a new world; it was as if we were a pair of savages till now and now that we had stepped onto this path, we were slowly acquiring the trappings of civilization.

We walked for about a mile along the path and reached our cottage. Everybody was fast asleep and we had to bang on the door for quite a long time till the manageress answered. The sight of two foot-weary wanderers with rucksacks on their backs so early in the morning left her amazed and speechless.

Very briefly we explained, 'We spent the night among the boulders on Hoverla mountains.'

Chamois, the wild goat of Europe

The lady almost fainted. 'How did you survive the cold weather and the rainstorm in the wilds of the mountain? Are you all right?'

'Not at all!' we responded. 'We are hungry, thirsty, frozen, exhausted and dying for lack of sleep.'

The kitchen was opened immediately and we sat next to the fireplace, which had gone cold by then. The cook woke up, rubbed her eyes, rekindled the fire and set about to boil some milk for us. We washed up with some hot water, ate something, wrapped ourselves in a bunch of quilts and went off to sleep before the other trekkers were up.

EIGHTEEN

*I*t was almost noon when we woke up. We went into the dining hall and found a group of trekkers eagerly waiting to hear about our adventure. We traded a lot of information. We heard about how a year ago a trekker had climbed to the top of Hoverla and got lost in a dense fog. Many of our fellow diners expressed their opinions about how and why we lost our way. From what we could understand, the reason why we got lost was that the road we'd left, thinking it was the road to Petros, was the right path to the Hoverla cottage. If we had consulted the map, we would have realized our mistake. We would have seen that the path to Petros was marked in red, and not in yellow! But in the hurry and worry of trying to reach the cottage, we'd not thought about this. The road to the Hoverla cottage had taken a U-turn only to avoid the impenetrable forest. The forest looked deceptively small, since it was well concealed in the folds and cracks of the mountainside, but in reality, it was very deep and covered a vast area and was quite impassable as well.

We decided to recuperate and recover our strength and spent the night resting at the Hoverla cottage.

There was a path to Petros from here; it was quite a

straightforward path without many ups and downs and would take only about six hours on foot. The path went through a pine forest, with many little streams and springs on the way. A couple of cottages, quite empty, lay on the side of the path.

'I think these are hunting cottages, used only during the hunting season,' Mirek observed.

The joy of walking was fully engrossing. The trees, the leaves, the fruits, the flowers, the soil, the water, the air, the sunlight, the shadows—these were now my very own friends. They and I were part of a huge family. But strangely enough, till a few days ago, I didn't know them at all, they were nowhere as close to me as they had become! With every step I took, their breath made me feel more alive; their pulse became my rhythm, which made the blood course through my veins and my body feel so light. That's why I felt such joy.

Mirek stopped suddenly in front of an abandoned hunter's lodge, below which was a picture-perfect pine forest.

I immediately understood the reason for his sudden stop. 'What have you found now? More raspberries?'

'No, no berries this time. I'll just walk into that forest.'

'Have you found the scent of some fruits?'

'Not fruits, no. Mushrooms.'

I sneered at him. 'Not those! What will you do with those things?'

'You wait at that cottage, just for a little bit. I'll have a look around and come back soon.' Mirek dropped off his rucksack and went into the forest.

The cottage had a wooden porch on all sides and its

two rooms were locked. I sat on one of the porches and stretched out my legs.

Just then it started drizzling. Mirek made his way back to the cottage, and by the time he climbed onto the porch, it had started raining hard. He held five round mushrooms and was really excited. 'Did you know that these are the finest mushrooms from our mountains? They are called hribi.'

While I was marvelling at the power of the sixth or seventh sense which told Mirek about the location of wild fruits, berries and now mushrooms, Mirek had started to cut the mushrooms into small bits. 'Bring out the stove and let's boil some water. We'll have to stay here for a while, thanks to this rain. We can eat here.'

'You want me to eat those mushrooms?! Not me! You can eat them all,' I said.

Anyway, I lit the stove and started to make some sandwiches for myself, and Mirek started making mushroom

Hribi: the king of mushrooms

soup, while it rained cats and dogs outside. By and by, the aroma of the mushroom soup drowned out all other scents. It was quite special, and truth be told, the aroma was so good, it had me salivating!

'Do you want a taste?' Mirek asked.

I put one spoonful in my mouth. What a wonderful taste! It had something that was absent from all other food that I'd come across. It was like the smell that you get deep inside a pine forest; it was like the aroma that wafts across your nostrils when a bright shaft of sunlight falls upon a wet forest road covered by a thick layer of small conical pine leaves. It was so tempting that I polished off half the soup, and since then I have remained a firm and dedicated fan of hribi mushrooms.

The rain showed no signs of slackening. All the sides of the porch were wet, and we hung up our rucksacks onto the walls of the lodge to prevent them from getting drenched once again. There was no place dry enough for us to sit. We watched a thin little mountain stream swell up with the rain water and run down the hill like a torrent, its clear water now coloured red.

Mirek said that we would have to drop our plans of walking to Petros in these conditions.

After a long time, the rain weakened a little bit. We looked at the sky and the state of the path and decided to abandon all ideas of walking to Petros. Instead, we wrapped ourselves in our raincoats and returned to the Hoverla cottage.

The people at the cottage had guessed that we would be coming back, thanks to the rain, but did not expect us to return in such a dry state. When we told them that we had feasted on hribi soup, they didn't believe us and their sarcasm knew no bounds. 'Of course! Of course! You must have found a hotel inside the forest!' said one of them.

The rains played havoc with our plans. We had to wait till two o'clock of the following afternoon for the rain to stop and the sky to clear up sufficiently for us to leave the cottage. We didn't go to Petros but went down the hill instead. At the foot of the hill lay a village called Luhy, which was just a few hours walk. That was our destination.

The path wended its way downhill. We entered a huge forest, which was quite unlike any that we had encountered so far. At first sight, our feeling was 'What have we got ourselves into now?' It was like entering a forest dated before human civilization, indeed before human history. It was like entering a fantasy world: in the depths of the forest, which covered hundreds of thousands of square miles, hidden behind the huge trees, lay colossal reptiles and bats of gigantic proportions; we felt as if the very trees were alive and that they were in reality unknown creatures that only looked like trees. They seemed to follow us furtively, behind our footsteps. We felt like we had entered a maze of stupendous size and proportions, from which there would be no easy escape.

This was the world-famous primeval forests of Ruthenia. In these huge forests, huge trees have been born and have died—man had very rarely stepped inside. Dead trees lay exactly where and how they had fallen; no woodcutter or any other person had touched them. Branches, twigs and leaves fell on the forest floor or onto the thick carpet of leaves and brush which lay above the floor; they die there and decay after death; over time, other trees grow on this floor. And so the cycle of birth and death continues.

It took us the whole afternoon to cross this forest. By the time we reached Luhy, it was evening. It was a tiny village, next to the Tisza, a fast-flowing river whose lively burbling filled the entire village.

The cottage was completely occupied, but the manager promised to find us some accommodation. He took us to a farmer in the neighbourhood, who made us comfortable sleeping quarters in a hayrick covered with straw and horse feed. His wife fed us home-made round buns. We clambered up a ladder to the top of the hayrick, and went to sleep listening to the Tisza telling us tales of her journey.

NINETEEN

The next day, we reached a small town called Rakhiv, from where we had planned to climb one of the high peak of the Carpathian Mountains, Pop Iván. The feeling of imminent rain, which had been threatening us the whole time we had spent in the Carpathian area, was still strong, so we had to stay in Rakhiv for a few days.

Then one day, the sun rose bright and golden. The forest smiled, the river shone and the villagers laughed and danced with every step. The sky, the water, the road, the village, the forest—everything told us to get out of the house and bask in the sun.

Without wasting any time, we loaded our rucksacks with food and other necessities, and hit the road again. We walked along the banks of the Tisza, the village and fields as pretty as the prettiest of pictures. Little fields of grass nestled on the lap of the hill, invited us to stop for a moment, lie down and roll about on their beds. The beautiful path and the sun-soaked day actually slowed us down!

Pop Iván was about as high as Hoverla, but it was not as wild. If we lost a path, we could find it again quite easily. And in any case, after our adventures in Hoverla, losing our way held no fear for us. We sat at the edge of the woods next to a stream, drinking tea and lying on the velvety-soft grass, enjoying the spectacular beauty of the mountains and not caring how time flew.

When we reached our cottage, it was dark. It was exquisitely beautiful, by far the prettiest cottage we'd visited. And its location on the hillside was also magnificent. When we took down our rucksacks and were signing in the register, we realized our error. This was a hotel; our cottage was another half hour's walk away.

The hotel and its location were so beautiful that we did not feel like going away. Mirek said, 'Forget the tourist cottage, we'll spend the night here.'

I asked the manager, 'Do you have a discount for members of the Tourist Club?'

'Of course, they just pay half the price.'

That was the clinching argument. We couldn't give up this great opportunity. We signed up and stayed the night at the hotel.

Next morning, we looked out of the window and were charmed by the sight. The owners of the hotel were really smart, they'd built the hotel in such a pretty place that whoever checks in for one day would surely stay on for five.

The Tourist Club cottages were very different. There was a strong feeling of transience about them, as if everybody has come just to spend a single night; everybody is planning to leave as soon as possible; everybody is thinking about the fields, forests and roads in the world outside. It's as if there is always an urgency to move on, to go ahead. The people we met, the cottages we stayed in—nothing could stand in the way of the irresistible urge to move on.

I sat in a chair by the window in the dining room, feasting my eyes on the glorious view, completely mesmerized by the beauty of the row upon row of blue-hued mountains and deep green forests.

I asked Mirek, 'Hey, shouldn't we walk about in this area around Pop Iván and explore it more thoroughly? We could make this hotel the centre point of our treks.'

Mirek said, 'I must confess that I would love to spend a few days at this hotel. Indeed, as a wanderer, this is quite an embarrassing confession!'

We had about eight days in hand for our journey to the High Tatras, so we decided to spend those days at Pop Iván, going out on daily walks in various directions, but returning to this hotel every evening.

Later that day, we took one rucksack instead of two, packed it with our waterproof jackets and some food. We wandered about the forests and hills, taking turns to carry the rucksack, until we reached a spring on the shoulder of a hill, when suddenly Mirek said, 'I think we'll find bilberries over there.'

An idea suddenly came to me and I said, 'Mirek, you're an experienced trekker while I'm still an amateur and although I don't have as much knowledge as you, I think I can smell hribi mushrooms in that forest there below.'

Mirek was excited. 'Bravo! Well done! Spoken like a true walker. Let's see what we can get from the forest.'

We went off by ourselves in two different directions. The ground under the trees in the pine forest was a thick carpet of dry leaves. I searched for hribi mushrooms in and around the leaves and in the surrounding bushes. But unfortunately, I couldn't find any. I was convinced that they were around there somewhere; it was only because I didn't know how to look for them that I couldn't find any, just as had happened when I'd gone looking for strawberries.

Feeling quite low, I was about to return to our path, when I suddenly noticed something peeping shyly at me from behind a tree trunk. I ran back and there it was—a pair of hribi mushrooms! I felt that now I could call myself a true trekker. Carefully, I picked up the pair and looked around. I could now see hribi mushrooms where earlier I had seen nothing.

Inside the forest, I found six more mushrooms and returned to the place where we had parted, only to find Mirek sitting on a stone next to the spring with a long face. He hadn't found even half a bilberry.

Mirek was a good sport; he was really happy that I'd managed to find hribi mushrooms. 'Now, you have graduated to an expert trekker.'

We returned to the hotel with our haul of eight mushrooms and showed them off to all the other guests. They were most impressed and congratulated us. 'In this area, you have to be really lucky to find eight mushrooms at one time,' they said. I felt really proud of my achievement, so much so that instead of one cup of coffee, I ordered two cups for myself.

We were talking with the others when an elderly gentleman joined us at our table. We'd chatted to each other before and we'd learnt that he worked in the railways, and had gone on a walking tour with his son during his vacation, and was staying at this hotel.

'How has your holiday been?' we asked.

'We're enjoying ourselves. How was your trip?'

'Splendid! We got eight large hribi mushrooms from the forest we visited,' I said.

'Really? That's great news! I hope you'll give us a taste when you cook them.'

'Of course, of course!' Mirek said. 'Where's your son?'

'He's carrying something quite heavy so he's fallen a little behind. He'll be joining us soon.'

The young man joined us just then, carrying a huge bundle on his back. His father helped him put the bundle on the ground and called us. One look and we were astounded. The bundle was filled to the top with hribi mushrooms of different sizes.

The gentleman smiled. 'I've accepted your invitation for tonight. But you must accept our invitation for tomorrow. You must come and feast on mushrooms.'

We accepted the invitation but felt like a pair of also-rans.

'Mirek, tomorrow we shall go to the same area that the gentleman and his son had visited today. Speak to him in Czech and find out from which forest he'd collected his mushrooms.'

'Nobody tells others such secrets. They keep it to themselves. I'll try anyway, but not with much hope.'

Mirek tried to extract the information from the gentleman in different ways, but without any success. We decided to travel in that direction the next day in any case and try our luck.

We spent the next few days diligently searching the whole area around Pop Iván for the storehouse of hribis that the gentleman and his son had discovered, but in vain.

The rail employee and his son spent the next couple of days cutting up the mushrooms into slices, drying them in the sun and packing them into tins for future consumption in soups, broths, omelettes and other dishes. They fed us mushrooms generously as well. One fine day, they left the hotel and went their way, without giving the magic key to the mushroom kingdom to anybody.

TWENTY

We were to leave for the High Tatras in just a few days. In my letter to Satyatbrata, I'd written that we should meet on 19 August at a place called Smokovec, in the valley of the High Tatras. We had never been to the place, and neither had he. We had planned to meet at the office of a company called Chedok. We had learnt of its existence from newspaper advertisements, but we had no idea how to reach its office. The only thing certain was that we had planned to meet between 10 and 11 o'clock in the morning of the appointed date.

Satyabrata had written in his letter that he would be waiting for us at the appointed place at the appointed hour. But his letter had reached us quite some time ago and we'd had no correspondence since.

We took a train from the Carpathian region and after a long journey, reached a village in the High Tatras at night. After spending the night there, we travelled onward and reached the small town of Smokovec when the clock was just about to strike 10.

We could find the Chedok office quite easily. Inside the office, we found Satyabrata standing in a corner, with his back towards us, studying a wall map of the local region with rapt attention. He had a rucksack on his shoulders and was wearing a thick pair of boots and a pair of shorts, showing off his muscular calves, thanks to his regular cycling.

Mirek looked at his legs and commented, 'Your friend will be an excellent walker!'

'Better than me, that's for sure,' I replied.

Satyabrata turned at our voices. 'Ah! There you are.'

After introducing him and Mirek, I asked Satyabrata, 'I didn't imagine that you'll come all dressed up as a trekker. Where's your cycle?'

'I've sold it.'

'Why?'

'I've travelled through many countries, but pushing and riding the bike has become boring. So, I have decided not to use the bike on this journey. I've come ready to walk with you.'

'Excellent!' Mirek said. 'You'll never get bored of walking, you'll see, even if you're walking alone in these mountains. That's where cycling loses out to walking. It doesn't matter how many countries you visit on your cycle.'

I agreed, 'Just like the hare losing out to the tortoise.'

Satyabrata had to agree with this sentiment.

We sat around a map and discussed our plans to walk in the High Tatras. It looked like we could cover the whole area in about seven days of walking. Although we had more time in our hands, we were unwilling to spend more than seven days here. There was a reason for this. While the High Tatras was famous throughout Czechoslovakia for its natural beauty, it had become 'fashionable'. In addition to walking tourists, others came to the place in large numbers only to spend a lot of money. As a result, boarding and lodging at tourist cottages and elsewhere was quite expensive. This went against the grain of walkers like us, whose ideal was to spend the least possible amount, and not to spend unnecessarily. So, we decided that it would be best for us to cover this region as speedily as we possibly could.

Our first destination on leaving Smokovec was Lomnica. It was quite close by and it had a Tourist Club cottage as well. We could not take a long trip that day. We had things to buy, and as our walks over the last few weeks had worn out the soles of our boots, they needed urgent repairs.

Lomnica was a couple of hours away. After a while, Satyabrata became pretty cheerful. 'The cycle had become a baggage; this is much nicer, I feel a lot lighter.'

'The rucksack is pretty heavy!' I exclaimed.

'It's now a part of my body, like a wing. Thanks to the rucksack, I'm now flying!'

'You're right; I feel the same way.'

We reached Lomnica, a small town with hotels, shops, cafes and picture shops filled with well-to-do tourists seeking luxury and delicacies.

'Many people have heard of the beauty of the High Tatras, but are unwilling or unable to take the trouble of climbing the mountain peaks. They come in droves to the small towns and resorts at the foothills, and return home to brag that they've travelled in the High Tatras!' Mirek sounded quite aggrieved.

We spent the night at the Tourist Club cottage and on the morrow, we were ready for our journey. We broke our fast with coffee and bread at a restaurant at the crossroads in the middle of the town, and had just packed our rucksacks and were about to leave, when the owner whispered something to Mirek.

Mirek turned to me. 'He wants to know if you would mind if he took photographs of you and Satyabrata.'

'Of course we wouldn't mind! We'd be really happy to oblige,' I said.

On hindsight, perhaps I overstated our happiness. The owner placed himself and his huge belly between Satyabrata and me, put one arm around my shoulder, the other on Satyabrata's, and got the picture taken. I had my doubts about how the picture would look. There is a story about this photograph, which we came to know of later and which I shall tell you about in a later chapter in this book.

The owner thanked us profusely, and said that all the trekkers stopped at his restaurant for a meal, but he had never been lucky enough to have *two* copper-coloured walkers in his shop. This would be a huge advertisement for his shop.

TWENTY-ONE

We hit the road the next morning. We had not planned on continuously climbing the mountain slopes right from day one, particularly since this was Satyabrata's first day of serious walking. In addition, the mountains in this region are made of hard granite, the paths of hard stones, with little or no trees or bushes; these are difficult hills to climb and are really taxing on a walker.

Our goal for the first day was Zelene Pleso, which means 'Green Lake', on the shores of which the Tourist Club had a pretty and charming cottage.

We climbed along the shoulder of the mountain, sometimes through green fields, sometimes through woods, sometimes across barren stony ground. Next to a stream, we found a large number of raspberry and red currant bushes, ripe with fruit. We dropped our rucksacks and filled our bowls with berries and red currants.

The trekker's meal on the first day on the road is always a little sumptuous. The rucksack is filled with good eatables. Our rucksacks had many non-trekker-like delicacies such as green peas and cauliflowers. In addition, we had bought cake and cream to celebrate Satyabrata's first day in the mountains. Feasting on such goodies helped to fill up our hearts and stomachs, and at the same time made our rucksacks lighter.

We found a little inn on the way, and we went in to have a coffee each. The inn was on top of a hillock and had a good-sized glass window, which commanded a magnificent panoramic view of the surrounding area. A gentleman was sitting on a chair by the window with a steaming cup of coffee in his hand. The other three chairs at the table were unoccupied and looked very inviting. We sat down on the three chairs.

The man introduced himself as Novak. We introduced ourselves.

Novak had visited the High Tatras many times. 'Every time I come here, to this inn, I cannot resist the temptation to sit by this window.'

'Why?' Satyabrata asked.

Novak asked him to move closer to the window, and said, 'Now look outside.'

All of us looked outside. The Tatra Mountains stood like a huge protective semi-circle around a vast wilderness, filled with stones and trees. Like a perfect picture framed by the window. We had to admit that the view was indeed spectacular.

Novak turned to Satyabrata. 'You've seen the grandeur? Now imagine you're a bird stuck inside a cage. This window is the door of the cage, closed and locked. The wide open world outside, the crystal-clear air outside, the wide blue sky, the mountain peaks, all of them are calling out to you, beckoning to you to come outside and join them.'

Satyabrata nodded in agreement, 'Yes, I can imagine that.'

Novak said, 'That is the game I play. For the whole year, I play this game. For the whole year, I am stuck in a cage in the city with shackles on my feet. My mind thinks of when I shall get my freedom and I can travel. I come here during my summer break and sit by this window to see for myself that time has indeed come to break my shackles and has opened the door of the cage for me to fly away and enjoy my freedom. Sitting here with my coffee, I was lost in thoughts. Talking to you made the sentiments clearer to me.'

Satyabrata said, 'We are all caged birds; we've got free from our shackles about a month and a half ago. But once we've finish our travels here, we'll have to think about returning to our cages.'

'Don't remind me of that. Sir, please don't remind me.' Novak said. 'I've just arrived today. I'm going now to spread my wings in the free sky outside. Goodbye, gentlemen!'

He paid for his coffee, put his rucksack on his shoulders and without further ado strode out and vanished round the corner.

Mirek said, 'I've met many holiday-mad people, but this one surely takes the cake!'

We finished our coffees and hit the road once more. The vast arid land was filled with stones and boulders, punctuated here and there by lakes and a few fast-flowing rivers, with forests of creeper pines on the river banks. We trudged along this path for the whole day. In the evening, we reached the end of the huge field and arrived at the foot of the craggy mountains we had seen in the morning. We found the green lake and our cottage on its bank.

There was still some daylight left, so we went out to see the lake. This was a stony land. On three sides of the lake rose steep walls of granite going up to the top of the mountain range. In the folds of the mountainside, where sunlight never reaches, huge sheets and blocks of ice lay spread like white blankets thrown higgledy-piggledy. The ice melted slowly, a little every day, and the melted water came down the mountainside to form the lake. There was so much ice in the folds of the granite walls that all of it does not melt in the summer. Come winter, and another layer of new ice falls over the mountain walls. The lake was always filled with water, summer and winter, and the excess water overflowed from one side as a stream. The water was crystal clear; perhaps the floor of the lake was made of some stone the colour of emerald, hence the lake was always a clear, bright shade of green.

After dinner, someone said that the moon has risen. Some of us came out of the cottage to look at it. It was so very cold that we couldn't stay outside for very long, but the sight of the High Tatras in moonlight was really unforgettable.

We had not noticed him so far, but there in the crowd was our old friend Novak.

Satyabrata went up to him. 'This wondrous sight will make a poet out of me. Standing here, one feels like bowing down to this grand mountain range.'

Novak did not take kindly to this. 'Such a sentiment does not suit a true trekker. However beautiful a mountain may look from below, its true beauty can be perceived only from its peak. The true walker understands that; he does not praise the mountain's beauty from the foothills; he climbs to its top!'

TWENTY-TWO

Next morning, Satyabrata woke up and said, 'You remember what Novak said yesterday? We must climb a mountain today, otherwise we won't be able to save face.'

We started climbing. It was a steep and difficult climb—paths made of broken stones, rough, ragged, hard and grey. This landscape had not the slightest resemblance to the sylvan meadows and greenery of the Lower Tatras. From time to time, streams born of melted ice flowed down the stony slopes; they could merely wet the stones, but could not make them green.

We climbed through these bare, unadorned, rocky paths and reached the spine of the range. Satyabrata looked below at the slopes and the valley and felt relieved. 'Finally! We've been able to preserve our self-esteem and can call ourselves true trekkers.'

We'd saved face all right, but the whole area was so covered with clouds, that we could not see the beauty from the peaks, which Novak had been so insistent about.

Satyabrata appeared to have taken to heart Novak's apparent slight on trekkers. He set a really fast pace. By three o'clock in the afternoon, we had reached our destination cottage, which we had planned to reach in the evening.

'Now I realize that we have a cyclist in our team...he runs while we walk!' Mirek joked.

'Beware! I am now a pure unadulterated walker!' Satyabrata responded.

The cottage at Skalnaté Pleso was very pretty, but none of us wanted to end our day's walk so early. We had tea at the cottage and set out for the cottage at Kamzik, about three or four hours away.

The road started descending and forests of green pine started reappearing. The clouds started to disperse slowly and soon we were walking in bright sunlight. The sun lifted our spirits, all except Mirek's, who was well-versed in the vagaries of the weather in the High Tatras. He looked serious. 'The weather signs are not clear. I hope we don't have to end our sojourn in the High Tatras in wet clothes.'

We reached the cottage in the evening; a group of fun-loving walkers were already there and had livened up the cottage with music and singing. This is not a very common thing in our experience and we really enjoyed it. Members of the group came and chatted with us. One gentleman looked at Satyabrata and me and said, 'I feel really jealous of the two of you!'

'Jealous! Why?'

'Look at me closely! I came walking in the mountains in the hope that a few days in the sun will make me nicely browned and tanned when I go back. Perhaps I have tanned a little bit, what do you think? But next to you, I look like a pale anaemic ghost!'

Another person asked us, 'Tell me honestly, how long do you take a sun bath for to get your tan?'

Satyabrata said, 'Actually, it's all a matter of timing. If you take your sun bath at the right time, you don't need to do it again and again. The day we are born, our mothers put us out into the sun for a couple of hours and that is that... our colour is fast for ever.'

The group erupted in laughter, which drew another person to our group. 'Hey, I know you people! I've seen your pictures!'

'Where did you see that?' I was surprised.

'Down at Lomnica. The shop is selling your pictures labelled as "Indian trekkers at Lomnica"!'

'That's one smart shopkeeper,' said Satyabrata.

There was nothing to be done about it, except take our hats off to the clever shopkeeper, a good businessman that he was.

The conversation kept us all entertained until pretty late. Early to bed was the normal practice at tourist cottages; here, for the first time in our experience, people were reluctant to break up the party, which went on till late at night.

Everybody wants to get to bed late but wake up early. I thought that if I wake up early, I can beat the crowd in the bathrooms. But everybody seemed to have the same idea. So many travellers had arrived the previous night that there was a big crowd waiting at the bathroom doors and it was quite impossible to wash ourselves. 'Waiting here will take a lot of time. Let's go to the spring outside the cottage,' Satyabrata advised.

The spring had turned into a bathroom with another big queue! Half the inhabitants of the cottage were waiting there with toothbrush, toothpaste, soap and towels of different sizes, colours and patterns. The ice-cold water almost froze our teeth, but we brushed with a great show of enthusiasm. We had a very truncated bath using the tiniest possible bit of soap and a few handfuls of that icy water. The bath left us feeling very fresh and energetic.

After breakfast, we started on our way to Poprad Lake. The High Tatras had many lakes, big and small, and Poprad was perhaps the best known amongst them. Our Tourist Club did not have a cottage there, but there was a large hotel. It would be more expensive to stay there, but we were keen on climbing one of the high peaks of the High Tatras and the best approach was from Poprad Lake. Also, everybody told us that since we had come all this way, it would not be befitting to go away without seeing the Poprad Lake.

We started on our way but after a while the sky started to darken and we began to worry about being able to reach Poprad Lake that day. Mirek quickly consulted our map and found that there was a hotel midway on the road. We decided that in case it started raining hard, we would take refuge in the hotel.

The rain held off, and at around one o'clock in the afternoon, we reached a spring from where we could see the hotel quite close by. We stopped there to have our luncheon of bread, butter and cheese—we'd run out of food by then.

Well, we had covered half the distance and we should be able to do the rest. With that thought, we finished our meal and started walking towards Poprad Lake.

After about half an hour, it started drizzling. We would not stop. We put on our waterproof jackets, covering up our rucksacks as well, and continued on our way. The drizzle turned into a shower, then into a drencher. Then came thunder and lightning and a deluge.

We left the road and took shelter under a large tree. Satyabrata had donned a large yellow waterproof jacket, as worn by cyclists, and sitting under a pine tree, he looked like a huge yellow toadstool.

We waited, and got wet, for an hour. We thought that we would perhaps not be able to reach Poprad Lake that day. In that case, we'd have to return to the hotel on the road and stay the night there. But the rain slowed down and our optimism came back redoubled. We left our shelter under the tree and started marching towards Poprad Lake with squelching shoes.

We walked for a couple of hours and had come a long way on our journey, and entered another region of rocks and stones. We'd climbed to the top of this rocky range when it started raining once again. There were no trees to give us shelter here—not even a blade of grass. We increased our speed thinking that perhaps we could reach some shelter sooner. It started pelting down now and this time there was no escape: our belongings and we were thoroughly drenched. The rain lashed at us from all sides and was driven by icy cold winds. All we could do was to cover ourselves up with our waterproof jackets as best as we could and continue walking.

'Remember I'd said yesterday that we will have to get wet on this journey?' Mirek said.

'Satyabrata, this rain is hellish!' I complained.

Suddenly, the rain stopped, and the clouds parted slightly to show us a bit of sunlight. We sat down on a large rock, took off our shoes and were squeezing out water from our socks, when we suddenly heard the words '*Dobrý den.*'

We looked around us but couldn't see anyone. Suddenly, from below the rock we were sitting on, a bone-dry traveller emerged, like a man emerging from a crack in a ground in a folktale.

He looked us over and in a voice full of pity, said, 'You must not get wet like this!'

Mirek was annoyed. 'You had found protection hiding under a rock. If you had been caught in the open like us, you too would have been drenched like a scarecrow.'

What the man told us was quite a surprise. 'There is no reason to get wet in these mountains. There are so many cracks and holes in the rocks that an entire army of trekkers can take shelter from the rain.'

Mirek was still smarting. 'We didn't notice any cracks in the rocks. We're visiting for the first time.'

'I am also coming for the first time. If you want to be a trekker, you must train your eyes first. If you're going to walk blindly, why walk at all?'

Mirek had to remain silent. After a while, he said, 'Anyway, what's done is done. Now all we want to do is get to Poprad Lake cottage as quickly as we can, and sit by the fireside. How far is the cottage from here?'

'I have no idea! I'm also going in the same direction, so let's go together.'

Though Mirek was a little irritated, very soon all had been forgotten and he started chatting gaily with the stranger, whose name was Steiner, and was quite an entertaining person.

We reached Poprad Lake in about an hour and a half.

TWENTY-THREE

Right on the lake was the massive hotel, virtually empty. After all, nobody was going to brave themselves travelling through the rain. Everything that a traveller could ask for to make his or her stay comfortable was available in the hotel. Of course, it was expensive, but for trekkers, the hotel had a huge room with about a hundred beds, which were quite cheap. You could even cook your own food if you wanted to.

We decided to stay in that room and made arrangements accordingly. Steiner also decided to stay with us.

We had very little food left with us; our rucksacks were almost empty. So, we had to eat at the hotel. We were struck speechless by the prices on the menu card; we decided not to stay at the hotel for more than one night.

It has been well said that man proposes but God disposes. Next morning, the whole place was dark and completely fogbound. We had planned to climb one of the peaks of the High Tatras, Rysy, from here. But the conditions clearly told us that no such journey would be possible on that day. Therefore, very reluctantly, we had to abandon our plans and stay on at that expensive hotel for one more day.

Charanik ★ 135

Peak of the Rysy mountain behind forest and stream

The four of us sat down at a table next to the fireplace. Someone at the next table was drinking tea. Mirek sighed, 'It would have been great to have some tea. It would have warmed us up in this cold weather. But the prices are sky high!'

I said, 'Let's go to our room; we can make tea in our spirit stoves.'

But nobody wanted to leave the comfort of the warm fireplace and walk across the cold and wet courtyard to reach our room.

Satyabrata said, 'I'm not leaving this fireplace. I have an idea!'

Satyabrata asked the waiter to bring us four glasses of hot water. He opened his rucksack and after some rummaging, brought out a tea infuser, tea leaves, sugar and lemon, spread them out on the table, and started to make tea. We had to praise him for his brains.

We made ourselves comfortable and started to sip our tea, when we heard someone at another table ask the waiter to bring them glasses of hot water. They had been watching us carefully.

Satyabrata was indignant. 'See, they've stolen my patented idea!'

Steiner told him, 'Don't get angry. Trekkers cannot be selfish about their ways of doing things. All the little secrets you know about living cheap and eating cheap should be shared with all the travellers that you meet.'

He shared his knowledge with us that evening. He really was an expert trekker. He told us that while most people walked about Central Europe in summer, the best time to go on walking tours is autumn. While it is true that it stopped raining and snowing when winter came to an end, but most people do not realize that it rains a lot more in summer than in autumn. Indeed, one cannot depend on the constancy of the weather in summer, while the autumn weather is a lot more dependable. Another important aspect was that many of the edible wild fruits and roots were available most widely during autumn.

Steiner told us that once he had spent one whole month walking in the Ruthenian mountains without carrying even a single piece of bread. Blackberries were available in such plenty that one could fill one's stomach with these berries alone. He had obtained all his sustenance from nature, of which the most important were blackberries, the roots (which the Czechs call 'peasant's bread') of a type of thorny bush, hazelnuts, hribi and other types of mushrooms. These are found in plentiful supplies in the hilly regions. He did not carry a spirit or wood stove, since there was a profusion of dry branches and twigs one can collect in the forest to make a fire; all one needed was a box of matches. When possible, in the evenings he would descend to the valleys, where it was not as cold as up in the mountains. He spread pine brush and leaves in a dry rocky clearing and made himself a comfortable bed for the night.

This was really inspiring. One could get really close to nature and travel at virtually no cost. Satyabrata said, 'I'd love to do this. But, sadly, our holidays are only in summer!'

The next day opened cloudy but there was no rain. We didn't waste time and very soon we were on our way to climb Rysy. The road was very steep, made from broken rocks. The peaks of the High Tatras were really difficult to climb; some were indeed considered inaccessible and could be tackled only by experienced mountaineers using axes and ropes.

Rysy was not that difficult. One could climb with some strong walking. On the other side of Rysy was Poland; we had been told that the view of Poland from the peak was very beautiful.

The higher we climbed, the foggier it became. Slowly, the sights started to disappear into the fog, until we were climbing enveloped by whiteness. Many trekkers had started to climb Rysy encouraged by the rain having stopped, but now they were looking despondent.

At the peak, we suddenly recognized a known face. It was Novak, who, standing on the shores of the green lake, had lectured Satyabrata that the beauties of the mountains are best seen from the peaks, and not from the foothills. He was climbing slowly using a stick for support.

Satyabrata ran up to him. 'Hello, how are you?'

Novak was very happy to meet us.

Satyabrata was intent on getting his own back. 'You still have the enthusiasm to climb to the top?'

Novak could not understand the trend of the conversation. 'Why? Is it far away from here? I thought we were going to reach it soon.'

Satyabrata said, 'You remember what you'd said to me: that the beauties of the mountains are best seen from the peaks and not from below? How far is that peak now?'

Novak understood the matter now and looked quite sheepish. 'I know. Truly, you can't see someone who's just 10 feet away.'

Fog resembling a bunch of cumulus clouds was still climbing up from the lower slopes and was about to engulf us and the peak in a white seamless cloak.

Satyabrata smiled. 'That's why I had said that the beauties

of the mountains had to be enjoyed from below.'

Novak looked down. 'True. Pride comes before a fall. I stand truly abashed.'

We saw Rysy through fog as thick and white as cotton wool. We were denied the sight of the famed hills and dales of Poland; we couldn't even see our feet. One cannot blame Satyabrata for praising the sights of a mountain while standing at its foot. After all, all the peaks he had climbed had been fogged out.

The rains did not hold off. When we descended from Rysy and reached Poprad, it started raining once more. We could not tell if it stopped raining at night, but when we looked behind the curtains at dawn, it was still raining hard.

There was no point in waiting at the Poprad cottage. We left our beds, freshened up, had something to eat, packed up and left Poprad Lake for the next step of our journey.

After a few hours of energetic walking, we reached Strba Lake and called it a day. We had covered almost the whole of the High Tatras, from the east to the west.

TWENTY-FOUR

We realized that the chances of the sky clearing and the rains holding off for the next few days were quite slim, and accordingly, we decided to move on to our next destination.

Mirek now made a request, which could not be denied. 'We've been to Slovakia, and we've also visited Ruthenia. We still have a few days of our vacation left, so let's go to my country.'

'Good idea!' I readily agreed.

Mirek came from Central Moravia, with a mountainous region in the northern part. He suggested that we travel in that area. Czechoslovakia had many mountains, and it had much to offer its city dwellers, as we had realized during our travels and while talking to the walkers we met on our way. If you are feeling tired, or quite energetic or just want a change of scene, all you had to do was to get out of doors, take a bus or a train. And hey presto! Within a space of two or three hours, you were in the mountains. Drink a cup of hot coffee or a mug of hot chocolate at an inn in the foothills, put your rucksack on your shoulders and start climbing. Walk till the end of the day, when you will find a cottage of the Tourist Club or a little inn up in the mountains, where you can spend the night. Walk about the next day, feast on wild berries which you've picked in the woods and return to the city in the evening, feeling like a new man, a giant refreshed.

Satyabrata had spread out the map and was studying it intently.

Mirek remarked, 'The maps say nothing about the beauty of the mountains of northern Moravia. You don't know the Czech language either; otherwise I could have recited some wonderful descriptions of the land from our literature.'

Satyabrata commented, 'Perhaps you can translate them for us. However, after studying the map, my feeling is that we should have taken a longer vacation.'

'How long?' Mirek asked.

'About as long as the mountain ranges in your country. I would have gone and climbed the Šumava peak in southern Bohemia. Then, you see these mountains along the northern and western borders of Bohemia. These continue along the northern border of Moravia, then through the north of Slovakia, along the northern part of Ruthenia, all the way through Romania. I would have walked this whole range, not leaving a single thing out. Only then would I have been able to claim that I have walked in Czechoslovakia.'

Mirek was excited. 'Great idea! Then promise me that we'll meet again, and walk from the Šumava and travel to Český les, Krokonse, Jesenike, Fatra and Tatra on towards the mountains of Carpathian. Wherever we run out of our vacation time will be the starting point of our walk the year after.'

I said, 'Why stop at the Carpathian? We can continue... Transylvania, Caucasus, Elbruz, the Pamirs, and finally the Himalayas. From there, we can drop quickly down to Calcutta!'

Mirek's hometown was in the middle of the plains of Moravia. We spent the night at his home, and the next day, we left for the mountains of northern Moravia, together with Mirek's brother, Pepek.

Pepek was very excited by the idea of going on a walking tour with two Indians. So what if we didn't have a common language? We could always find a way to communicate. The four of us shouldered our rucksacks and put our collective best foot forward.

Our step was to take a train to Bruntál, a tiny little town. From its name, we guessed that there was a spring nearby. True, there was a natural spring with water flowing out of a crack in the ground. Pepek said that the spring water was famous for its therapeutic qualities.

Sadly, we couldn't spare to visit the spring or taste its waters. We had to catch a bus to the mountains and were pressed for time. We bought some food and other necessities and boarded our bus. Our destination was Karlova Studánka, which also indicated that there was a natural spring in the vicinity.

Mirek said that this place was a spa, with many natural hot springs and that the waters were used for the treatment of a number of diseases, thus attracting many rich and sophisticated people. There were many excellent hotels and places for dancing and other entertainment. In short, a most unsuitable place for walkers.

On reaching Karlova Studánka, we started our onward

journey, leaving behind the various attractions and temptations of civilization. The path led us into a deep forest, from where the sky was completely hidden from our eyes thanks to a thick canopy of green leaves; even the darkness seemed to have a green hue. In front of us walked a forest guard in a green uniform, which was such a good camouflage that only his movements betrayed him to us.

We caught up with him. He was an elderly man, simple and straightforward in mind and body. We fell to talking and in a few moments, we were chatting like old acquaintances.

'Where are you going?' he asked.

'We plan to spend the night at Ovčárna. Then we plan to walk around the area around Jesenike.'

'You've chosen a very good time of the year to visit Jesenike. It's the end of summer and the beauty of the leaves on the trees at Ovčárna is a sight to behold. The deciduous trees are getting ready to shed their leaves. It's as if a painter has used his brush to carefully colour the leaves.'

'Which way are you bound?'

'Half an hour uphill after Ovčárna is Visoky Hole. There's a big, dense forest on its right. I live inside the forest.'

Mirek exclaimed, 'I know! You must be the guard of the Frantiskova forest bungalow! I've often seen blue smoke rising into the sky from deep inside the forest. People say that there's a cottage in a secluded spot inside the forest.'

'That's where I live. Drop in if you're going that way. I can treat you to some venison.'

As we were speaking, we noticed that the forest guard was falling behind and periodically we had to stop or slow down to let him catch up with us.

Impatiently, Mirek asked, 'Why are you walking so slowly?'

The guard had a long and hearty laugh. 'I'll tell you. For many years, as a matter of fact, for more than 40 years, I've walked on forest roads and mountain paths at various speeds, sometimes slowly, sometimes fast. I used to walk as fast as you, faster than you in fact. I'd jump and leap and run and scamper up the hills, and then I would pant. I'd lie on the grass, spread my arms and rest for a while. And then be up and on my way again. Sometimes I've walked all day, sometimes all night, thanks to my work. The speed at which I walk now... this is my discovery after years of experience. At this speed, I will never tire. I can walk as far as I want, for as long as I want...at the end, I shall be just as fresh as when I started.'

We found this really insightful, but Satyabrata said, 'That may be fine for you, but I'm feeling restless, my feet can't walk slowly.' He dragged me along and we went ahead. Mirek and Pepek kept the forest guard company and fell behind, talking to each other in Czech.

After a couple of hours, we came to an open place in the forest, where stood the Ovčárna cottage, nestled against the mountain slope in a charming field dotted with bushes and dwarf pine trees. The cottage had a stone floor raised from the ground, with wooden walls and a wooden roof. There were two large, comfortable bedrooms, which could accommodate almost 50 people. The mouth-watering aroma of mushroom soup wafted in from the adjoining dining room.

Here the forest guard bid us goodbye and made his

Ovčárna chalet, with the Praděd peak in the background

homeward journey, walking at his own unhurried pace. We made ourselves comfortable, grabbed our bowls and started to fill our stomachs with excellent mushroom soup.

The sun had set a long time ago, but darkness was still some two or three hours away. After dinner, we stepped out of the cottage. A group of boys and girls from Pepek's school were staying at the Ovčárna cottage. Pepek brought them along and introduced us. All of us sat down on stones next to the dwarf pines and started a singing session—songs of village life, songs of grass cutters, songs of farmers, songs dear to boys and girls. Moravia is famous for its folk songs; whenever a few of her children get together, they break into songs of their motherland.

Under the open skies, on the mountain slopes of Jesenike, looking at the pine forests around us, listening to the songs of the children of this land—the real beauty of the Moravian mountains was slowly unfolding in front of our eyes. The tall, arrogant solitude of the High Tatras had no place here. Neither did the huge expanse of the Low Tatras or the grandeur of the Carpathian forests. Instead, there was a wondrous peaceful beauty, which gently touched our innermost being.

In the darkness of the late evening, the singers fell silent and we took our leave. With full hearts, we returned to the cottage and took to our beds for a well-deserved rest.

TWENTY-FIVE

Our destination for the next day was the peak of the Praděd. The path snaked up the steep slope. The forest had ended and now the road made its way through rocky ground, dotted with bushes.

Pepek said, 'The old forest guard was right, you guys walk too fast!'

'If you want to be a good walker, you must go fast,' Mirek countered.

Pepek said, 'So, you won't pay attention to the words of that man of great experience? You want to tire yourselves out?'

Mirek said, 'We'll pay follow his advice when we are older. Now we can get tired, rest awhile and then walk some more.'

Pepek was nonplussed. We also did not have the patience to walk any slower. We had got so used to our pace that we had lost the patience to slow down. Sometimes we'd look at poor Pepek and slow down, but very soon, our feet became restless, as if they wanted to fly! What could poor Pepek do? He had to come at our pace like a reluctant schoolboy.

We followed the serpentine path and finally reached the top of Praděd. It was so windy up there that it virtually forced us to the huge 'View Tower' at the top. Mirek said, 'It always blows like this up here.'

Shivering in the bitterly cold wind, we reached the view tower. The side of the tower facing the wind had been severely eroded. The wind seemed to shake the tower even unto its massive foundation.

Satyabrata said, 'In Bengali, there is a word (ঝোড়োমূর্তি / jhoromurti) which means "storm-stricken figure". This is the first time I'm seeing it in real life!'

Our feet had gone black in the cold. Thankfully, there was an excellent coffee shop on the ground floor of the tower, which was a lifesaver.

Pepek joined some of his school friends who had come to the tower. We brought out some food and sat down with our coffees. Suddenly, we were joined by an excited Pepek. 'My friends have heard that there are lots of hribi mushrooms in the forest below the Alfredova cottage. They are going there. I'm going with them. When are you joining us?'

Mirek said, 'Pepek, you make friends easily, but you part with them just as easily! So, you are leaving your Indian friends?'

'I can't help it, the hribi won't wait for me! They'll be around for a while and I can meet them again. Please don't mind...it's the call of the hribi. We'll meet at the Alfredova cottage.'

Very soon, Pepek and his friends vanished down the slope. We too left the view tower.

The road from Praděd to Vřesová studánka was quite easy, without many ups and downs. The entire roadside was filled with bilberry bushes. I'd never seen so many bilberries in my life—the whole mountain was blue!

The whole area was very dry, with a strong wind blowing all the time. Therefore, lighting a fire of any kind out of doors was strictly forbidden. Trekkers were given specific instructions not to light fires to cook their food anywhere in this open meadow; a mere spark could lead to an out-of-control forest fire. We met a few people on our way, who, Mirek said, were forest guards who kept a very strict lookout for anybody lighting fires in this area.

When we reached the cottage at Vřesová studánka, there was still a lot of daylight left. This was the result of our walking even faster after Pepek had left us. We were supposed to stop here for the night, but our feet did not want to rest. Some unknown urge drove us forward—it propelled us to go ahead until night fell.

We did not enter the cottage but walked on. The road went gently down the hill towards a wide wooded valley, beyond which was another range of hills. That was the border. On the other side was Germany.

We reached the forest after an hour and a half. It was not very dense but filled with very old trees—so old that even birds seemed to shun them. The trunks had lost their bark; the branches were shorn of leaves. The ground was strewn with large broken branches, twigs and other remnants of old trees. The whole forest looked in utter disorder.

I said, 'We'd seen something like this in the primeval forest of Ruthenia. Remember, Mirek?'

Mirek said, 'This place is called Červene sedlo. Many people call this the primeval forest of Moravia.'

Suddenly, there was a shout from Satyabrata. 'Quicksand!'

We froze. I looked down and saw that my feet were also sinking into the mossy ground, which was covered with algae, moss and thorn bushes.

'Nothing to worry about,' Mirek said. 'This is the funny thing about the moss in this forest; if you stand on it for some time, it looks like your feet are sinking into a patch of quicksand. Look closely, your feet have not really sunk even a bit.'

'Strangers to these parts will certainly panic!' remarked Satyabrata.

'You're quite right! Maybe they will run away from the forest,' said Mirek. 'Since you mentioned strangers, let me tell you a story. This happened two winters ago. In winter, the whole area gets blanketed in snow and looks very different. Grass, moss, trees, bushes—everything gets covered in snow. Only dry branches and leafless trees stick out like skeletons from the covering of snow. That's when expert skiers come to Praděd. This place is not for beginners or casual skiers—inexperienced skiers are prone to crash on the slopes and break their limbs. But for expert skiers, these are the best slopes in the whole country.

'That winter, two Slovak boys reached the top of Praděd. It was snowing very hard. The view tower was completely covered with snow and looked like a giant pillar of sugar. The coffee shop was a chock-a-block; skiers from everywhere were crammed into the room. The two Slovak boys had a cup of hot milk each and left. Somebody asked them where they were going, and they said 'Červene sedlo'.

'Although it did snow that day, it was quite clear from time to time. But a little while after the two boys left, a sudden fog blanked out everything. The fog didn't clear; nor did the two boys return. By and by, it became dark and it started snowing very heavily.

'The owner of the coffee shop was worried and sent out a few people to search for the two boys who had come from another land. They put on their skis, tied torches to their waists and went out braving the snow. But searching in the pitch darkness of night in the heavily snowing conditions was not at all easy. Where will they search? How will they find the way? It was all to no avail. The search party came back; the two boys did not.

'The next day broke bright and sunny. The snow shone blinding white. So much snow had fallen through the night that if the two boys were lying dead somewhere, there was no chance of finding their bodies under the thick blanket of snow. People searched for news of the boys from all the nearby villages, cottages and lodges—there was no news; they had not reached any of these places of refuge. It was clear that they were buried in the snow somewhere in this area.

'Winter went by; the two boys lay interred in their unknown snowy graves. When the first warm breeze of spring began to thaw the ice, their perfectly preserved bodies were discovered in this forest. Around them lay strewn many half-burnt matchsticks.

'This is the danger of getting lost in the snow. The

tiredness, the lassitude you feel when you are freezing is very dangerous. The flames of a few matchsticks are insufficient to fight the cold. You struggle to keep your eyes open and your mind and body just need one thing—sleep. You don't feel the cold any more; all you want to do is to wrap the blanket of snow around you and go to sleep. Trying to stay awake is a huge fight against all your urges; sleep is a blessed relief. But once you give in to the urge, that is your final sleep, the sleep from which you'll never wake up. Death in the snow is not really the end of life as we understand it—it's like a deep sleep from which there's no waking up.'

Mirek stopped.

After a few moments of silence, Satyabrata said, 'That is scary. I promise never to come here in winter.'

We walked right up to the edge of the forest of Červene sedlo. It was almost evening, so we returned through another path in the forest. It was fun to walk that day.

Walking had become a passion for us. The few more days that we spent in Jesenike followed the same pattern: we'd start out early in the morning and continue till the long summer afternoon faded into the darkness of evening.

Pepek was waiting for us at the Alfredova cottage; our vacation was also coming to an end. So, we had to return without any further ado.

Those who have travelled in the mountains, particularly on foot, know the sadness one feels while bidding adieu to them. Saying goodbye to them for the last time was heart breaking, I can't even begin to express our feelings. It was like saying goodbye to a world of freedom, only to return to jail.

From Praděd, we walked along the ridge of the Vysoky Hole mountains, the Ovčárna cottage to our left. It was a long ridge which took us fully two and a half hours to cover.

On the eastern side of the ridge was barren land, a downhill slope without a single tree, without a single leaf, with strong wind whistling as it blew. There was no chance of rain—the wind just blew away any cloud that wanted to tarry there. The lack of rainfall made the eastern side of Vysoky Hole totally barren and inhospitable to any stray seed that may fall there.

By contrast, if you look at the western side of the ridge, your eyes rest on dark green forests—so beautiful, so wonderful to see. All the clouds from the eastern side cross the ridge and drop their moisture on the western side. The result: mile upon mile of green pine forests. From the exact centre of the pine forest, a thin line of blue smoke rose into the area, shaped like a question mark. Though we couldn't see its source, Mirek said that the smoke was coming from the kitchen fire of the secluded cottage of the forest guard we had met earlier.

We left the cottage behind us, the promise of venison was tempting, but we couldn't give in since Pepek was waiting for us impatiently at the Alfredova cottage.

He had been waiting for us at the cottage for two whole days. Pepek's friend did find the promised storehouse of hribis, so he was very happy. He had already cut the mushrooms into slices, dried them in the sun and packed them into tins. He handed one tin each to Satyabrata and me and said, 'Souvenirs from Moravia!'

I was very happy. 'We really missed you when you left us, but this wonderful gift you've given us more than makes up for it!'

It would take us another three and a half hours of walking to reach the railway station. We ate something quickly and went on our way, with Pepek joining us. After a non-stop bout of walking on comfortable roads and crossing the dense forest in the foothills, we reached the Rýmařov station. From here, our team was to break up: Mirek and Pepek would return home, while we'd go to Prague.

Our last day together was another golden sunny day. There was a smile on every lip, a laugh in every eye. It was like the first day of a holiday. It didn't feel like the day for our return to everyday life, but the first happy day of a journey. But, sadly, this was not the case—Mirek and Pepek went home, and the two of us went back to Prague.

At Prague, we emptied our rucksacks and packed up our suitcases. There was a tear in my eye when I looked at the thin and crumpled state of our rucksacks that we had carried on our shoulders for so many days; these had been so plump and healthy till now. While putting on my tie after so many days, I felt as if I was putting a noose—the noose of civilization—around my neck.

'Shall I tell you what I feel?' asked Satyabrata.

'What?'

'If, rather, I had been an Arab Bedouin...'

The author getting ready for his day's journey

ACKNOWLEDGEMENTS

I wish to thank a few people, without whom this book would never have seen the light of day. First, my thanks are due to my old school friend, Soumya Chakravarti, who introduced me to the author's children. Second, I must thank Dr Urmila Ganguli and Mr Mitendra Ganguli, the children of the author, and owners of the copyright to the original work and the visuals used in this book. They have supported this project with energy and excitement, and have responded to my requests for permission and use of visuals with great enthusiasm.

I also wish to acknowledge that all the photographs in the book were taken by the author's wife, Mrs Milada Ganguli, who also drew the images in the book (all except the sketch of the chamois, on page 105, which was drawn by Mr Asit Roy). The pictures are from the archives of the copyright owners, Dr Urmila Ganguli and Mr Mitendra Ganguli.